HORSE, GROOM, BLACKSMITH *Saratoga Race Course, 1978*

Racing Days

Photographs by Henry Horenstein

Text by Brendan Boyd

AN OWL BOOK

HENRY HOLT AND COMPANY

NEW YORK

This book was first published in 1987. Since then, a few of the numerical facts mentioned—yearling prices, jockey records, etc.—have changed. Because we believe the book reflects a certain moment in time, however, and is more concerned with the race-track state of mind than with its statistics, we have decided to leave the text largely in its original state. Some photographs have been added and changed, all in the spirit of the original edition.

—Brendan Boyd and Henry Horenstein

Henry Holt and Company, Inc.
Publishers since 1866
115 West 18th Street
New York, New York 10011

Henry Holt ® is a registered trademark of
Henry Holt and Company, Inc.

Library of Congress Catalog Card Number: 95-76519
ISBN 0-8050-4293-8

A Pond Press Book

Art Direction: Lisa DeFrancis Studio, Boston
Design: Lisa DeFrancis, Melissa Cohen
Production: Amanda Freymann and Mary Reilly
Darkroom Technicians: Porter Gillespie, Andrea Raynor
Copyediting: Diane Taraskiewicz
Printed in Hong Kong by Palace Press
Typeset in Sabon

Henry Holt books are available for special promotions
and premiums. For details contact: Director, Special Markets.

First published in hardcover in 1987
by Viking Penguin Inc.

First Owl Book Edition—1995

10 9 8 7 6 5 4 3 2 1

Opposite:
Track Entrance, Keeneland, 1977

THIS BOOK IS FOR
MR. AND MRS. JOSEPH C. BOYD—BB...

AND TO RACETRACK PALS—
CHARLIE, DAN, GREG, LYNN, MICHAEL,
RUTH, AND OMAR KHAYYAM—HH.

Racing Days

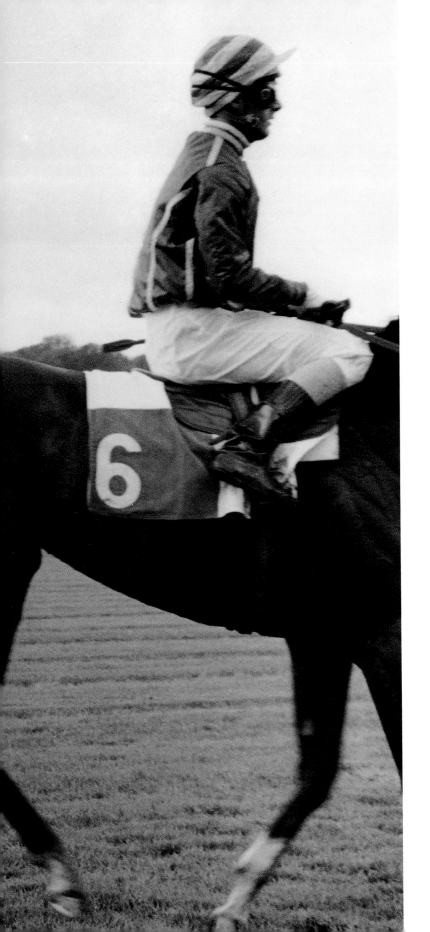

FROM PADDOCK TO POST *Hippodrome Saint-Cloud, 1994*

PADDOCK AFTER THE LAST RACE *Hippodrome Saint-Cloud, 1994*

Perfection

IMAGINE SOMEONE imagining a perfect day at the track.

He would want good weather, evocative surroundings, pleasant company, even if it was only his own. He would require sporting races, with large fields, at true distances. There would be one significant race to focus his enthusiasm, preferably late in the card. The crowd would be large, but not smothering; enthusiastic, but not indiscriminate. He would win, but wouldn't need to. If he lost, he would get close, always get a call. If he won, it would be by stealth, on worthy horses, with straight bets. To win by luck is to cede a significant part in it.

He would go to a major track, rent a small house, settle in for a while. His perfect day might be his very first.

He buys the *Racing Form* the night before, walks to a small store, ten blocks down. He passes the neat lawns, the Turtle-Waxed Fairmonts, neighborhood life. It reassures him, though he wants no part of it. The streets are dark, soundless, except for an occasional fox terrier, or the odd radio in an upper-story window. He feels safe, insulated, reverted, as though transmigrated onto a Frank Capra stage set.

He handicaps on the wraparound porch, in a wicker chair, under a hunter's moon, listening to the crickets, drinking Schlitz, peeling oranges. All his favorite horses are in tomorrow. Winners leap out at him, like apparitions. He circles their names. The town is silent around him, innocently asleep. A moth bats against a bare light bulb. The night seems boundless, thick with ambiguity. He figures the last race, smokes a small cigar, then goes upstairs to bed, falls asleep quickly, dreams of horses.

He wakes early. A breeze is blowing the curtains around the room. Children's voices rise up from the street. He puts on linen pants, a Breton shirt, red socks. He walks to the track for breakfast. He sits on the Clubhouse veranda, watches the workouts, reads the paper, eats French toast, turns his face languorously to the sun.

He goes to the lake for a swim, reads a book (a Balzac novel, perhaps, or A.J. Liebling). Then he walks to town for lunch, to a battered place where only racetrackers venture. He has another breakfast, for the idea of it, and an egg cream. It's seventy-five degrees, cloudless, with a faint breeze from the east. The afternoon stretches out endlessly before him.

He walks to the track at noon and meets a woman outside the gate, a mysterious, charming, sympathetic woman, who looks a bit like Ida Lupino and a bit like Francoise Dorleac. She's never been to the track before, but relishes the prospect.

The track is fast, the crowd fervid yet deferential. Musicians circulate. The jockeys pass on their way to the paddock, tapping their whips. They follow. They watch the saddling, the instructions, see the horses onto the track. They have a box in the grandstand, near the finish line. They hurry to it after betting. The infield is full of flowers, the sky an absolute blue.

He wins every race. No, not every race. More races than he's ever won before. His horses come from far back. The crowd screams for them. Their silks catch the perfect sun. His companion wins also. They eat hot dogs, drink celery tonic, point things out. Everything seems inevitable.

They cash their biggest bets on their last two picks—an unbeaten two-year-old, and an English shipper on the grass. The first goes wire to wire. The second rallies to win by open daylight.

They walk to an old hotel, sit in the garden, drink kir royales. The sun goes down. They have dinner in a small Italian restaurant, under a grape arbor. They review the afternoon, and other matters.

They retrace the town's dark streets, walk past the flawless lawns to the yearling sales. The moon is full. They wander among the dark barns, look into the horses' eyes, check their lineage. An elderly groom offers them a peppermint. They see faces from the afternoon, famous and otherwise. It all seems connected, a never-ending thing. The world feels very far away.

They leave at 10:30. The auctioneer's voice follows them into the night. They stop at the small store for a *Racing Form*, then walk down to the track. It is completely lit up. They stand at the fence looking in. She leans against him. He opens the *Form*. More of his favorites are running tomorrow. It could go on.

Lures

PEOPLE WANT TO KNOW how we "do" at the racetrack. "How do you do?" they always ask.

They mean the money, of course. People always mean the money. Do we win? How much? How often? They're hoping to grasp our motives.

We tell them we win sometimes, lose sometimes; on balance we're a bit behind. We hope this mollifies them, but don't expect it to. We ready the standard aphorism: "The best thing in the world is to win at the racetrack. The second best thing is to lose at the racetrack."

They nod at this, but don't buy it. It's too abstract, too enigmatic. We're tempted to elaborate, but resist. We hold our ground.

Gambling defines the racetrack for nongamblers, as sex defines love for nonromantics. It's the obvious peg for those who lack third eyes.

The truth is far more chaotic. For confirmed racetrackers, the gambling is just part of it. Four elements combine to lure us to the track: the horses, the sport, the life, the gambling. Each has its devotees, though gamblers predominate. Real racetrackers make no distinctions.

The horse part needs no explanation. Look at this picture.

Someone I know saw Affirmed at Del Mar. His handlers were late bringing him to the paddock. Everyone was worried. Then they saw him approaching in the distance, from the ocean, the mid-afternoon sun shining off his back. He looked, said my correspondent, "like God." Not *a* god. *The* God.

The sport part is equally apparent. Athletics without competition is just exercise. It's keeping score that gives it edge. Racetrackers keep score devotedly. They don't just want to see horses, they want to see *horses*.

The life part is somewhat more elusive. You have to look for it. It's what draws royalty to the track, and stumblebums. It's the fantasy—what happens around horses.

The gambling part everybody knows about. It's the only sport whose spectators are participants. Money is, as Wallace Stevens told us, a kind of poetry.

Would we go if there was no gambling? No. But nongamblers should draw no solace from this. We wouldn't go if the other elements were missing either. Some would. But when have some ever been us?

COOLING OFF *Saratoga Race Course, 1978*

Groom

THE GROOMS TAKE CARE of the horses. Owners stop by, trainers make rounds, but the grooms are always there, hands on the stock.

They wake at five with the horses, alone together in the dark. They walk down the shedrow, peer into each stall. A horse may have cast itself—rolled on its side, been unable to rise. Lungs fill quickly; death comes quietly.

The groom feeds his horses—oats, barley, mash, vitamins. The mix varies with the individual. Some horses are good "doers," down every bit. Others are finicky, and pick at their tubs. The groom knows the differences, feigns impatience at them. He changes their water, checks for cuts, swelling, signs of fever. He saddles some for the training track, walks others under the shedrow, clucking to laggards, giving them slack.

He "catches" their stalls, replacing old straw. It's their carpet, and also their bedding. It must be kept clean, to guard against infection. He cleans feet, wraps ankles, ices legs. He soaps horses returning from workouts, curries them, tells them stories, whistles them tunes.

Around eleven, he goes to lunch. At one, he goes to the races.

He brings runners to the paddock and helps saddle them. He watches them race, perhaps bets on them. He leads them back, win or lose, to the barn, washes them, walks them in circles, until they're cooled. He congratulates them, or consoles them. He believes they're his.

He has favorites of course, but doesn't let on.

After the races he's off, goes into town, to a movie, to the track rec room, as long as there's someone tending the horses. He drinks a beer, chats with other grooms, plays canasta. He sleeps on a cot in the tack room. He's always near.

Great horses have their own grooms. Three good horses share one. The slow or crippled may be ten to a boy. Competence varies. Illiteracy is pandemic, drunkenness not uncommon. The pay isn't much, even at the top, though winning grooms are often tipped by grateful owners. Some hope eventually to become trainers. Others are content where they are. It's their life, the horses. Many drift from stable to stable, track to track, mood to mood. They take other jobs, but always return to the track. Many are now women.

You see grooms walking their horses to the post, chatting in groups under the grandstand, standing in betting lines fingering a shank. You don't think about them, hardly notice them. They're a little ragged, a bit apart. They seem embarrassed to be seen there, at their clothes, at *their* grooming—all the things they don't care about. They move closer to the horses then, blend in with their shadows.

Grooms brag on their horses, imagine they'll run well, hope for their safety, revel in their triumph. A groom leading his horse into the winner's circle can hardly contain himself, often doesn't try to. They share the moment with others for the camera, but are alone with it back at the barn. It's complete then, the satisfaction. They know who's done what.

Don't fall in love with a horse, grooms are told. How do you not? You fall in love in your mind, in your imagination. It happens when you're not looking. The thoroughbred stirs everything without trying to, with its stillness, its inscrutability. Can you care for them without succumbing? Can you save yourself?

Losing a horse bludgeons all grooms—partially to a claim, completely to death. It disorients them. They're embarrassed grieving deeply for an animal. It's not supposed to feel as bad as it does.

There will be others, others say. There are others already. It's unseemly, as if the heart could legislate itself. They go on. It's their job. They have to, and want to. They've been prepared for it. It's there every day. The relationship is tenuous; only the bond is ineradicable.

GROOM APPLYING BANDAGES *Saratoga Race Course, 1985*

Workout

THE REAL WORK gets done in the morning.

The horses head for the training track at dawn, to prepare for specific races, or long campaigns. They're athletes.

Good horses are exercised more often than they're raced. The competition is crushing. They must be ready for it, but not overworked. Mediocre horses are raced into shape. They have just so many runs in them. They must win a check with each.

Workouts vary according to assignment. Distance runners gallop, sprinters do speed work. Beginners are drilled from the gate, veterans are kept continuously on edge. There's an air of pious self-aggrandizement to all of this, the suggestion that subtle variations in fine-tuning matter. Trainers keep elaborate charts of training schedules, justifying their approaches, and thus themselves.

The training track at dawn is a stunning apparition, an action painting of a presumably vanished world. Dozens of horses gallop alone, or in tandem, at varying speeds, to varying purposes. Necks extended, legs churning, they are models of exertion and facility. Outriders parade through the clinging mist, clockers hold up the sagging rails. The place is humming, yet eerily tranquil, like a medieval market inside a Fabergé egg. You see instantly why people go on the track, and why most of them stay there. You realize, too, why they consider this the *real* part.

Jockeys do some of the riding—for important horses, or important stables. "Getting out in the morning" is how they make their contacts. But exercise "boys" do most of it. Some are mediocre jockeys supplementing incomes. Others are kids in training for the races. Most have failed to make it in the afternoon. They grew too big, or drank excessively, or had some barely visible flaw in their technique. They're paid fifteen to thirty dollars per ride, depending on its purpose. Some work exclusively for large stables, others hustle for mounts. They never speak of themselves as "exercise boys." They say, "I get up on some horses for Mr. Whittingham."

Skilled exercise riders share many traits with successful jockeys. They have strong arms and soft hands, big egos and great courage. They also have "clocks" in their heads. Trainers want their horses worked just *so* fast. The good boy hits this time on the fraction.

It's an appealing sort of life. It's colorful and competitive, involves riding horses and wearing cowboy clothes. It's dangerous, and, who'll deny it, a bit disreputable. The workday ends at ten every morning. It's almost like being a jockey. It just isn't.

Morning at Santa Anita. Daybreak with palm trees. Racing suggests dissolution to most people, and thus a knee-jerk association with nightlife. It's surprising then how early racetrackers rise, how wholesome their allegedly profligate life has made them. Every morning promises a clean slate. The earlier they meet it, the more virgin the beginning.

This photograph shows a workout about to begin. The exercise boy, in the helmet, prepares his move. The trainer, in the cardigan, gives telepathic encouragement. The horse, eager to race, fights the bit. Small pieces of the track are tossed carelessly toward the sky.

WORKOUT *Santa Anita Park, 1986*

Clocker

ALL HANDICAPPERS CONSIDER SPEED. Some grow obsessed with it. It's measurable; you can assign it a number. Once established, it should repeat itself invariably, like clockwork.

The speedboys develop formulas to measure it. They award so many points for outside posts, so many for encumbering head winds, so many for negotiating turns. They add for weight, subtract for rider changes, multiply by Woody Stephens' social-security number.

It doesn't work. Nothing works. Horses aren't computers. They run just fast enough to win, or just slow enough to finish an inexplicable sixth. Just because they *can* run a mile in 1.35 doesn't mean they *want* to.

Such reversals don't discourage the speedboys. They consider all setbacks atypical, regardless of their frequency. It *should* work, after all—look at the figures!

If race time distorts, imagine practice time. Some horses just goof their works away. Others are overly serious, morning glories. But workouts never want for chroniclers; the speedboys can never have too much data.

These men are clockers. They haunt the track every morning, six to ten, training hours. They time as many horses as they can. They work for the *Racing Form*, or for the track, or for God knows who. They know most horses by their markings or their mannerisms. Horses they don't know are identified by spotters. They help each other, splitting works, comparing times. They speak of "catching horses," but it's really time they're trying to catch.

Everything is scrutinized at the track. Any nick might be an edge. Conspiratorial tones predominate, even in neutral matters, friendly settings. Good works are often masked and times questioned. Drills are held surreptitiously, on private strips, or before dawn, to cash bets, or hinder claims. It's the racetrack equivalent of midnight moving.

Every public work appears in the *Racing Form*. Impressive times are set in bold type. Significant works receive lyric annotation: "Cure the Blues is kept on edge." "Estrapade showed a high turn of speed." "Last Tycoon is rounding into form."

Twelve seconds per furlong is the standard. Bettering that, over distance, flutters hearts. Recent works are included in the past performance charts. A radical work strikes the horseplayer like the stab of love. "Oct. 10, Bel, 4 F fst: 44.4 h.," which translates "October tenth, Belmont Park, four furlongs, fast track, forty-four and four-fifths seconds, handily." This is punching the proverbial hole in the wind.

Some horses run back to their works. Most don't. Still, workouts can be instructive. They're the entire book on first-time starters. Injured horses signal recuperation in the morning. You can tell a lot about great horses from their works. You can't tell anything about mediocre horses from anything.

Speedboys love the works. They need to believe in something; it might as well be numbers. They don't realize handicapping isn't *that kind* of science. "Speed handicappers," says Leroy Jolley, "are guys with eight dollars in their pockets."

Some photographs are like novels, or the beginnings of novels. The details of this one are suggestive, and mysterious. It's late in the morning. Scores of horses covered the track earlier; now there's just one. Two clockers are timing it. They inhabit separate boxes, are dressed differently, display contrasting attitudes. Yet they hold their stopwatches identically, eye them with matching skepticism. One is seated, the other stands. One uses notebooks, the other a clipboard. The late morning sun is poking over the grandstand. The track's name appears in type, lower right; then again, in flora, upper left.

Make up your own explanation.

TIMING A WORK *Keeneland, 1985*

Timelessness

TIME DISAPPEARS at the track. It's meant to. It could be any hour, any day, any century. It always *seems* to be noon, midweek, mid-summer—1937 perhaps, or '38. We've left work early, hocked our Benruses, gassed up the Dusenberg. Pale sunlight lies lightly on the infield. Soft breezes brush the pliant tops of its trees.

Nine-race days replicate our time here. In the first race we greet the world, in the second get acquainted with it. In the third we ask it questions. Races four through nine carry maturity to the grave. Adulthood. Middle age. Reassessment. The end in sight. One last chance. Here's your hat.

Winning the first race lets us play with *their* money—though there's much to be said for bailing out at the end. In between is where our lives get lived. The shadows lengthen. The crowd grows quiet. But even the end has no real time in it. In this particular life, there's always nine more tomorrow.

For full-time gamblers, time loses more than its context at the track; it cedes all relevance. Post time is one. Tuesdays are dark. What else matters? They've turned their backs on the alleged real world, preferring a place where time can't get at them.

Backstretch workers seem even more immune. They're always around the track, even when they're not. The horses are their clock, their reference point. Soon they forget another world exists. They ignore elections, earthquakes, Eurobond rates. They talk only of horses, of fractions, of payoffs. They've wrapped themselves completely in this narrow world, made it enough.

There's something wonderful about this, and something awful too. It's passion worship; context denial. It's the perfect recipe for making time disappear.

The life resembles that lived in all undergrounds—by acrobats, boxers, gypsies. The horsemen rise at dawn, feed the horses, walk them, groom them, clean the stalls. They take them to the races, bring them back, cool them, make the rounds, break at sunset. They go to town, play pool, drink beers, talk to each other—about horses. They sleep in the tack room, watch TV, read the *Racing Form*, listen to the stalls. Every day. Around the clock. Around the calendar. Only the tracks change, and the towns surrounding them. The time is a constant.

Here is a portrait of no-man's hours at the track. It's late morning, any day, any season. The chores are finished. The training track is closed. First post is two hours away. There's nothing much to do now except sit around and wait, and think about the first race, and get your money ready. It's no particular time really, just racetrack time.

SHOESHINE STAND *Saratoga Race Course, 1978*

Trainer

TWENTY-FOUR hours a day, 365 days a year.

They reach the barn before dawn, roust an exercise rider, walk a cripple, repel two jockey agents. The first-time starter needs new shoes. They hit the training track, school a two-year-old, breeze the grass horse. They fire a drunken groom at eight, scan some X rays, file entries with the racing secretary. An owner appears unexpectedly at ten, a roofing contractor with two $5,000 claimers. He wants his hand held, wants to tell everybody how *he'd* do it. That's forty minutes right there. At eleven they catch up with some paperwork, ship a filly to Pimlico, advance a hotwalker a hundred. At noon they grab a B.L.T. and a boilermaker. First post is one.

They saddle five horses. None win. Owners are consoled, disappointment masked, jockeys are given instructions they're incapable of following. They return to the barn at six, feel the runners' legs, searching for heat. They haggle with a feed salesman, check tomorrow's schedule, leave at seven—after fourteen hard hours on the track.

They'll spend the evening massaging the accounts, reading the condition book, worrying. They'll make two calls to the barn, accept three calls from it.

It follows them everywhere. The schedule consumes them. It's no life for one who imagines any other.

The idealized trainer is a man with a stopwatch, chewing an alfalfa stem, staring at the sunset. He is Barry Fitzgerald, horseman incarnate. In truth, the horses are often the least of it.

Trainers must do everything, most of it commonplace, generic scutwork. They could be running a laundromat.

They come from everywhere—from ranches in Wyoming, from tenements in Canarsie. There's no formula. Some are trainers' sons; others bluff their way onto the track. They walk hots, become grooms, rise to assistant trainer. The aggressive ones eventually strike out on their own.

They run public stables or serve one owner, have sixty runners or one invalid, own their own or merely supervise. They make it up as they go along. Trainers' licenses aren't hard to come by. Most tracks have stalls to fill.

They must scramble until they catch a break. They charge thirty to eighty dollars per day, per head, depending on where they operate. They take ten percent of each purse. They're drawn to the uncertainty of it, and the possibilities. Some are manic, some calm; all are obsessive. All love horses, despite the con. They draw their satisfaction from the odd moments: the training track at dawn, the grandstand at sunset, winning one at the wire.

This is the entry room, a place of enforced camaraderie. It looks like a hiring hall in anthracite country. These unromantic-looking gentlemen are trainers. They're studying condition books, searching for spots. They have five different looks, but just one attitude. Most working stiffs dodge tension; these guys seek it. It's their drug. They spend all their time looking for one thing, the same thing all racetrackers are looking for. They're looking for *the* horse.

TRAINERS ENTERING HORSES *Fair Grounds, 1977*

Thoroughbred

THE DAWN HORSE, evocatively named, roamed Europe and North America seventy million years ago. This was eohippus, our horse's earliest ancestor. It stood twenty inches tall, about the size of the contemporary fox, and had toes instead of hooves.

The dawn horse was slow to evolve. Mesohippus adapted its teeth to grazing. Parahippus grew taller. Merychippus developed an arched neck. Pliohippus had longer legs for speed. By the Pleistocene epoch, one million years ago, the family (Equidae) had found its true vessel: *Equus*, the sole surviving genus. Modern species of *Equus* include the donkey, the zebra, and the wild Asian onager and kiang.

As horses evolved, they migrated from North America over now-vanished land bridges. During the Ice Age and its attendant floods, the strain vanished from the Americas. Stone Age horses inhabited only Africa, Asia and Europe.

The horse was one of the last animals to suffer domestication. It was first tamed by Asian nomads almost 4,500 years ago. Different civilizations isolated different traits, developing strains to satisfy specific needs. They bred strong horses for hauling, agile horses for hunting, fast horses for racing, bellicose horses for killing their neighbors. Horses didn't return to America until 1493, when Columbus brought a handful on his second voyage. They didn't return en masse until 1519, with the conquistadors.

The Indians had never seen horses. They coveted them instantly, and were soon trading with the Spaniards for them. Many Spanish horses fled or strayed, returned to the wild, began roaming the plains in vast herds, mimicking their forebears. All horses now living, except the nearly extinct Mongolian wild horse, are descended from tame strains.

Today, there are at least sixty breeds of domestic horse. The Arabian is the oldest, the thoroughbred one of the newest. The thoroughbred was developed in England less than 250 years ago.

During the reign of Charles II, oriental stallions were imported to the British Isles, to replenish stocks depleted during the War of the Roses. Three of these sires proved so dominant that today every living thoroughbred descends from at least one of them. They're the foundation males.

All three came to England chimerically.

The Darley Arabian was discovered in Syria in 1704 by Thomas Darley, the British consul stationed in Aleppo. A four-year-old bay with a white blaze and three white feet, he was a horse of unprecedented elegance.

The Byerly Turk was a spoil of war. He was captured by a certain Captain Byerly when England took Buda from the Turks in 1686–87. Byerly rode him at the Battle of the Boyne, a gesture of grandiose disdain, before sending him home to England to stud.

The Godolphin Barb's ancestry is more fugitive. He was called a Barb because he resembled the horses of Morocco's Barbary Coast. But nobody really knew where he came from. He was bought by Lord Godolphin from Edward Coke of Longford Hall, Derbyshire, in the late 1720s. Coke allegedly found him in Paris, pulling a water cart.

The thoroughbred often achieves seventeen hands now, or five and a half feet in human terms. It can weigh 1200 pounds and has a twenty-four-foot stride when running. It sees only shadows, never colors; but its nose surveys the landscape for miles, its ears detect whispers across canyons. Its normal temperature is 100.6 degrees Fahrenheit. Its blood is thicker and warmer than other horses'. It's a force of nature, transformed into an industry. This force is what draws us to the track, even if we don't quite realize it: this animal bond—this soulful physicality—this tribal memory—this *equus*.

HEADED TO WINNER'S CIRCLE *Saratoga Race Course, 1994*

Favorites

FAVORITISM IN BETTING is a transient state. Several horses may hold it until the windows close. A horse may be favored in one race, ostracized the next. It has to do with money.

Emotional favoritism is a more steadfast notion. We go to make memories, and to summon them. Our vision is by definition selective. It has to do with longing.

Here are my favorites, from the first forty years, for what it's worth.

Horse: John Henry. So many deserve remembering: Secretariat, whose Belmont was definitive; Kelso, who won every other Saturday; Silky Sullivan, who made belatedness respectable. But those are accomplishments, these are preferences. John Henry made a *Boy's Life* rise from mediocrity, hamming his way through every furlong of it.

Jockey: Braulio Baeza. Jockeys defy affection. They disappoint too often, and rarely atone. But a few make up for everything with their stylishness. Baeza was masterful and aloof. He always looked like he had something better to do, but was postponing it to ride just one more winner.

Trainer: Angel Penna. Trainers are like movie producers—essential, but anonymous. Few make lasting impressions. Penna has won at every level, on every continent. He looks like an Argentinian welterweight, dresses like Douglas Fairbanks, has both ends covered.

Eastern track: Saratoga, because time has forgotten it.

Western track: Santa Anita, because it has palm trees and Valentino's ghost.

Foreign track: Longchamp, because no matter how much you lose there, you're still in Paris.

Long shot: Key City. $107.20. July 14, 1967. My first hundred-dollar horse, the second-best horse in an indifferent nine-horse field, the inexplicable overlay of the century.

Short price: Chronic Town. $4.40. August 26, 1970. My first $200 bet, at a time when I didn't have $200.

Comeback: The day I entered Suffolk Downs with two dollars and left with twenty six; a teenage survivalist's trial by tote board, my personal version of Outward Bound.

Streak: The faultless afternoon at Saratoga when I picked the first six winners, forgetting momentarily that losing was an option.

Upset: The first time I went to Auteuil, taught myself *Racing Form* French on the Metro, walked right in and picked the first winner, and finished the day 300 francs ahead.

Race: The Kentucky Derby, unsurprisingly, and thus surprisingly. The idea of it transcends the race itself, of course. But when they play "My Old Kentucky Home" my throat gets narrow.

Month: May—Derby month, shortsleeve time, spring, a fresh beginning.

Type: Closers, with class, and courage, and a story.

Anticipation: The wait (captured perfectly in this picture) for yet another racing day to begin.

Realization: That your horse is about to move forever to the lead.

Inspiration: Two indomitable horses battling nose by nose to the wire.

Salvation: Winning, winning big, winning continuously, a hot streak.

SHEDROW *Monmouth Park, 1986*

Windows

THIS IS THE BETTING RING, without the bettors, the way nobody ever sees it. It looks like the operating theatre in a North Korean prison camp, or the room where Gary Gilmore boxed his last exacta.

Can you imagine it teeming with gamblers?

Give it a try.

Betting windows once implied specificity. There were $2 win windows, $10 place windows, doubles windows, combination windows—a window for every purpose, every sum. There was even a $100 "room," a confessional-sized cubicle with straphanger panelling into which the high rollers ducked to feign propriety.

Such categorization had clear advantages. It hastened the service, and reinforced prejudices. Everybody at the $2 window looked like they saved elastics. Everybody at the $100 window looked like they'd killed Jimmy Hoffa.

Of course it also made life harder for the distracted—people with more important things to worry about than: "Am I in the right line?"

I once went to the $50 window at Belmont to buy a ticket on a 9–1 shot. I bought the ticket and rushed away; I apparently had something important to do.

The horse won and paid $20.40. It made me feel very smart and very rich, the way every bet is supposed to make you feel. I got $510 for my $50 bet. That is, I would have gotten $510 for my $50 bet if I'd really gone to the $50 window, which I didn't. Where I'd really gone was to the $20 window, where I'd bought one ticket, handed the clerk a $50 bill, then walked away without my change, because there shouldn't have been any change, because I was supposed to be at the $50 window, you see.

I got $204 for my ticket, minus the $20 I bet, minus the $30 I didn't bet, but left at the $20 window as a sort of tip. This left me with a $154 profit, which felt curiously like a $154 loss, profit and loss being even more nebulous concepts at the racetrack than anywhere else.

Such mistakes are no longer possible. You can still bet a horse you didn't intend to, but you have to work much harder at it. And you can correct your error if you catch it in time.

All bets can now be made at every window, and also cashed anywhere. No more heady trips to the cashier's lair out back, those little jaunts to the fabled land of triumph. Winners no longer line up in self-satisfied segregation, like spelling-bee finalists, swapping modesties, looking blasé. Now you can cash in any line. Where's the kick?

In theory it's a much more convenient system—unless you're trying to bet $50 straight, and get caught behind a grandmother from Altoona cashing thirty-six show tickets for her garden club. Which you always do. So in practice it's a much less convenient system. But the computers like it.

Last year, $12 billion was bet at North American tracks. All flowed through windows like these, to be accepted, and some returned, by dyspeptic mutuel clerks. What are mutuel clerks like? Imagine Islamic Jihad running the post office.

GRANDSTAND INTERIOR *Laurel Race Course, 1985*

Truths

WE LEARN the same things over and over at the track. Every insight seems fresh on rediscovery. Such as:

You shouldn't go in the winter. The spectacle becomes a routine in the cold; the fantasy turns into an ordeal. The horses grow shaggy coats to warn us off.

Form is the all-abiding mystery. Horses go in and out routinely; nobody knows why.

The track is a closed system—the backstretch, the betting lines. It creates the illusion of an orderly universe.

If you stand up the track, the outside horses seem to be ahead. If you stand down the track, the inside horses have the edge. You can cash side bets on this illusion. It's best to stand a little in front of the finish line, halfway back, slightly elevated, in the sun.

Sometimes you mispronounce a horse's name for years, misread it, and nobody tells you. Other times you find out what a name really means, and wish you'd known earlier. It could have changed things.

Tractors rake the flat track between races. Water trucks dampen it. Lines of groundskeepers remove stones from the turf track, patch holes, walk the course.

To bettors, it often seems there are only two types of horse: front-runners who can't last, and closers who run out of track.

When you meet someone you've taught to handicap, they've always retained a few of your moves.

The best feeling is when you like a horse beforehand, have it figured, get a price, stick with it, see it win.

If you don't have the last winner, you don't have to hang around to cash.

No movie captures it. They get the racing parts all wrong.

Many people bring folding chairs to the track, plunk themselves in front of monitors, stay there all day. They never see a live horse.

The caller sees best. He sits in a small booth, high atop the grandstand, memorizing names and colors all day long.

The least likely people reveal racetrack connections, keep secret caches of *Racing Forms* in their garages.

Short-priced first-time starters are the best bets. Word gets around.

Particular races remain always in your memory. (An April afternoon at Longchamp, last race of the day, standing on the finish line. The field emerges suddenly from the fog, eighteen horses, one rallying boldest on the outside, in brilliant yellow. Is it mine? Yes, and past me in an instant, decisively toward the wire, sending me out onto Avenue de l' Hippodrome a winner.)

Watching many major races in one day is like watching no major race on any day.

Every bettor remembers getting shut out on a winner. Nobody remembers the losers they've missed, though there were more.

The more money you have, the more you must bet to get the same kick, and the less a winning day really means to you.

Certain races you know are unbeatable. Allowances with six fast sprinters, which any horse can win. Routes with fourteen cheap maidens, which no horse can win.

The first white horse registered with the Jockey Club ran at Saratoga a few years ago. It looked only a bit whiter than most whitish horses, but was genetically unique. Naturally, I bet on it. Naturally, it ran last.

The first time anyone sees the jockeys they say, "Look how tiny they are." Jockeys battle their diminutiveness counterproductively. They drive big cars, wear big jewelry, hang around with leggy babes. They seek association, get contrast.

Old racehorses often make friends with one another, grow

disconsolate when separated. There's one retirement farm for them, in upstate New York. It boards a few dozen pensioners.

Horseplayers check their *Forms* throughout the race. Does their horse *usually* run like this? Has it ever been this far behind and won?

Occasionally, a jockey gets caught with a battery. "Buzzers" give horses a slight jolt, shock them into running faster. Riders risk perpetual banishment by using them.

Breeding theories seem like the detritus of some other sport, with their hobbiest terminology, their genetic formulations, their tinkering.

All horses can be insured. The premiums are five to seven and one-half percent of their worth, so only the most valuable horses *are* insured.

Trainers and owners sometimes enter more than one horse in a race. A bet on one horse in an "entry" is a bet on all. Beginners love to bet entries; they'd rather back two slow horses than one fast one.

Any hit over a ratio of 600:1 attracts the attention of the I.R.S. They take your name right at the window. Certain men, with certain looks, will cash your ticket for you, surreptitiously, for a fee. They're called "ten-percenters."

An indecisive horseplayer will listen to any argument, give any twit his ear. The determining factor could come from any source.

The one thing you never do on the backstretch is abuse a horse. Transgressors are made to pay.

Every racetrack has a press box. They're best avoided. The air in them is thick with canned prep-school cynicism, that defensive knowingness that's really diseased naivete.

Thoroughbreds are sexually compelling. That's the unspoken part of it.

The excuses of horsemen are generic, and vague: "He wasn't himself today," "He couldn't grab the track." The excuses of bettors are equally generic, but specific: "That rider can't ride," "That trainer can't train."

If you buy one of those little souvenir pencils, you never have to wonder which track you're at today.

Some speculators trail grooms right up to the windows, stand behind them, to hear how they bet.

The track kitchen is a spirited place, homey and soulful. It's like the plant cafeteria in a Pat O'Brien movie. The help gathers there at 10 A.M., over beers. They've been up six hours already.

The simplest system: Stick a pin through the program, cover to cover. Play every horse whose name the pin penetrates.

All jockeys are called boys, regardless of their sex, regardless of their age. Asterisks denote apprentice jockeys in the program. For this, they're called "bug boys."

Certain bettors have to have a winner. They'll bet half the horses in a race to get one; they don't care how much it costs. They have to flash that ticket; they have to cash.

A fire is the worst thing. Hundreds of horses die in them every year. Yes, they do return to burning barns.

The last day of the meet is called "getaway day;" everybody's packing to move on. Don't go. It's like eating in a restaurant whose kitchen has closed.

The "overnite" lists the horses for tomorrow's races. It's a mimeographed sheet, available at the racing secretary's office. Get one, even if you're not going tomorrow. It'll make you feel as if you are.

The racetrack empty, viewed from the grandstand, up the track, suggests every dream worth imagining, whether discredited, or still unknown.

21

Hot Walker

THE THOROUGHBRED, racing, covers forty miles every hour. Exercising, it moves almost as quickly. If stopped, and kept motionless, it becomes chilled, pneumonia sets in, followed by death.

So it is critical to keep the perspiring horse moving. This is the job of the "hot walker."

All hot walkers used to be human. They were the official insignia of the backstretch—long files of imperfectly matched pairs, man and horse, circling the shedrow, temporarily linked by leather shanks. It was a task often grumbled at, yet secretly revered, like dreaming in motion, for who was walking whom? It was *the* entry level job at the racetrack.

Now machines do much of it—machines like the gangly device seen here, this rueful caricature of low-tech ineffability, looking like an abandoned ride at a bankrupt amusement park. A motor is at its center. Four horses may be lashed to its spokes, then turned slowly in tight, precise circles, like a water-wheel in reverse. Once horses provided power; now they're provided power.

Automation has spared the backstretch for the most part. There aren't that many jobs machines can eliminate, and the labor costs couldn't stand extensive paring. Where the machine age has intruded, though, its incongruity is this chilling.

Some riddles: Do horses ever become entangled in the works, or rebel at their bondage to stalk against the trend? Have any been forgotten by their handlers, and left to spin for hours, like Little Black Sambo's tigers?

Who knows? What is known is that idle hot-walking machines are sometimes used as makeshift clotheslines.

The source of this picture's power is problematic. The hyperbolic muck is a clue, as is the gulag fencing, and the all-pervasive drear. They brand the landscape inaccessible, as forbidding as a strip mine on Mars.

But that's not really it.

The horses are rebelling; the gray openly, the bay more tentatively. They look long since cooled. But that's not it either.

Try this: these horses are alone, shackled, mechanized, where once they were unfettered, random, accompanied. They inhabit the worst of all possible worlds: alone, yet still manipulated.

MECHANICAL HOT WALKER *Northampton Fair, 1985*

History

Horses were first employed in war, then in war's logical extension—sport. Races were carded in Babylonia, in Egypt, in Syria. We know this from the tablets. Horse-drawn chariots embellish Eighteenth Dynasty Egyptian art.

The earliest racing manual was composed in 1500 B.C., by Kikkidis of Mitanni, a Hittite figureman.

The first documented chariot race appears in the *Iliad*. Achilles arranged it as part of Petrochus' funeral. First prize: one lady.

Chariot races were introduced to the Olympics in 680 B.C. In the games of 642, men first raced on horseback. The Greeks loved racing, dropped bundles on it. In *The Clouds*, Aristophanes savaged Pheidippides, a dissolute stripling who bankrupted his father with bum tips.

But the pastime really took hold in Rome, among those most dissolute of blind-stabbers, the emperors. Tarquinus Prisius initiated annual racing in the Circus Maximus. Under Caligula, chariots competed from dawn to dusk. Professionals appeared, peasant types with strong whip hands, hot for celebrity. Claudius was an incurable high roller. Nero, said his biographer, Sueto-

nius, "had from his childhood an extravagant passion for horses; his constant talk was of the Circensian races." Still, Domitian was the absolute topper; he staged a hundred contests daily during his reign.

Caesar brought racing to Britain in 55 B.C. His medium was the speedy Roman horse, bred principally in North Africa. In 1174, Henry II built the first track specifically for horseracing, at Smithfield, outside the gates of London. Mounted horses competed over a four-mile course, the former chariot-race distance. The first recorded race for money occurred during the reign of Richard II (1189–99). In it, "divers Knights" negotiated a three-mile course for "forty pounds of ready gold."

The first annual meeting was held at Chester in 1512. The winner received a wooden ball with a floral design, the sport's maiden trophy. James I hastened the rise of English racing through his sponsorship of Epsom and Newmarket. Charles II, the true "father of the British turf," frequently rode his own horses to victory.

Charles' representatives established the sport in the colonies. Richard Nicolls, New York's royal governor, sponsored America's first formal meeting in February 1665, at a two-mile course on Hempstead Plains. Nicolls called his venue Newmarket, after its English antecedent. Racing spread quickly to New Jersey, Pennsylvania, and the Carolinas. By 1680, there were five tracks in Virginia. The first American strip specifically for thoroughbreds was the Union Course, built on Long Island in 1821. The first extended race meeting was held at Saratoga in 1864.

There seems always to have been racing, and its adherents. It is illimitable, and so are they. This horse's head, for example, could easily adorn some florid Byzantine antiquity. This groom, minus his adornments, could just as easily stand picturesquely beside him.

STARTING GATE *Linzay Downs, 1977*

Claimer

CLAIMING RACES are the markdown bins of the racetrack. Horses entered in them can be bought on the spot, cash on the barrel, like at Loehmann's. Their trainers may regret losing them, or not. They take their chances.

Horses don't run in claimers unless they have to. A race's claiming price, and its purse, are roughly analogous. No trainer enters a $50,000 horse in a $10,000 claimer. He'd lose it. No $10,000 horse runs in a $50,000 claimer. It couldn't win. A lot of maneuvering goes on in the margins. Trainers drop sore horses to dump them, lower fit horses to cop purses. The trick is to separate the motives. Free-market realities keep claiming races competitive, and bettors active. Successful trainers run their horses where they belong.

Most races are claiming races—forty percent at the best tracks, eighty percent at the worst. There are simply more bad horses, as with everything. There are $250,000 claimers at Belmont, $2,000 claimers at the fairs. Most claimers are in the $5,000 to $15,000 range. The quintessential race is the $7,500 claimer.

Only trainers racing at the current meet can claim a horse. Claims must be filed fifteen minutes before post time, dropped in the box. Competing claimants shake for it. The claimee takes any purses won during the race. The claimer takes the horse, as is. More than one trainer has claimed a dead horse.

Succeeding at claiming is how most trainers survive, snatching runners, losing stiffs. They play their hands coyly, employing informants, spreading rumors. Some trainers are never claimed from; they'll claim retributionally from those who do. Others are raided continuously; they don't know what they're doing.

Horses, too, have fixed claiming patterns. The fragile and cantankerous are rarely claimed. The consistent and promising are taken regularly. Every trainer thinks he can improve another's horse.

Most claimers are just working stiffs really, horses who've lost it, or never had it to begin with. Those who specialize in them are similarly afflicted.

In 1943, Hirsch Jacobs, from Brooklyn, a former pigeon racer, claimed a two-year-old named Stymie for $1,500. In five years he won almost a million dollars with him. Since then every trainer quotes Stymie to you—the beau ideal of bloodstock empires on the cheap. "See, it can happen," they tell their short-pursed patrons. It's part of the dream.

The dream's dark side is the afflictive descent. Once in claiming races, horses have prices on them. The fashionably bred and reproductively intact are spared the killing slide. They're sent to breed when their racing days are done. The mongrel and the barren keep right on running, drifting lower, shifting owners, having the final dollars squeezed from battered legs. You see them at the cheapest tracks—knees swollen, floating along on bute, raced every third day, until something gives irreparably. It's like seeing Joe Louis in wrestling trunks.

BACKSTRETCH *Northampton Fair, 1985*

Farrier

No FEET, NO HORSE.
No SHOES, NO FEET.

Thoroughbreds' legs go spontaneously. There's no telling. So their feet get obsessive attention. It's all that can be done.

Soles are cleaned daily, hooves are oiled constantly, bunions are rubbed with pine tar, blisters are packed in river mud. Trainers touch the feet every chance they get, feel the ankles for heat, probe the heels for tenderness. Horses are walked in endless circles, or posed, as here. Their stride may be a hair off, their balance suspect. Watch the trainers as the horses leave the track; their eyes rarely leave the feet.

Shoes are replaced as often as necessary, or oftener. Racing plates are made from aluminum, cost thirty-five dollars a pair, including installation, which takes about twenty minutes.

Radical changes sometimes move horses up. Special shoes suit special purposes, fit special needs. Bar shoes protect quarter cracks. Raised bars guard against scraping. Block heels preclude slipping. Jar calks help in the mud. But mostly it's a matter of busy work, like switching jockeys or adding blinkers. It's something to try.

The man with the hammer is a farrier, a blacksmith. Except for veterinarians, horsemen say, only farriers make steady money at the track. This isn't exactly true—it's a representational jibe, against the riskless professions that thrive on all their hazard: the feed salesmen, the horse transporters, the equine insurers, the dentists who file down jumbo molars, the carters who haul the manure away. Horsemen depend on them, and resent them. They charge, but take no chances. Horsemen wouldn't change places with them, though; they'll take the risk.

Every track has a few farriers. There's more than enough work. They wander the shedrows like archaic meter readers, tending to the feet, spreading the news. They're the unofficial communications network of the backstretch. It's an inherited profession, it should be done mechanically by now, but can't be. It's too primitive to be updated.

Everything about this picture is out of time. The battered tool box, the leather apron, the three figures, their three poses. Nothing in it couldn't have been true a thousand years ago.

BLACKSMITH *Monmouth Park, 1986*

BETWEEN RACES *Santa Anita Park, 1986*

GROOM *Northampton Fair, 1985*

Vet

ONE IN FIVE racehorses loses a month of training each year. Nine of ten lose a race to injury. Less than half compete each season. One percent die from race-related injuries.

They're overbred, overtrained, overraced. They look so powerful, they couldn't be so fragile. Yet they are. Keeping them fit is the biggest part of it.

Half a ton of weight lands on one leg at a time. Each leg averages three inches around. A thoroughbred's ankle is narrower in places than a human's. It's an evolutionary tradeoff. They're not as durable as they once were, but they're twelve miles an hour faster.

Some of their injuries are predictable. Most two-year-olds buck shins. Many bow tendons, temporarily, or permanently. Lots of horses run down, shredding their heels against the track surface. Then there are the prosaic ailments—canker, thrush, ringworm. They're as susceptible to virus as infants, as prone to arthritis as octogenarians.

More exotic problems attack the legs. They develop bone spavin below the hock joints, skin lesions on the knees. They grow osselots on fetlocks, suffer quarter cracks and curb and laminitis. Or they just plain break something, and survive it, or don't. The thoroughbred's ankle has twenty-two separate bones.

The secret defects disquiet horsemen most—the tendency to expire for no good reason in their stalls. Many of these afflictions are emotional.

Bleeders rupture nasal veins from exertion. Nervous horses wash out in the paddock, or swallow their tongues, or suck air obsessively. Stall-walkers pace endlessly, weavers sway until they drop, cribbers gnaw their stall doors to the nub. Some horses are compulsive eaters, others just pick. Lovesickness strikes routinely, as does jealousy. Loneliness is a constant. Goats and ponies serve as surrogate companions.

Veterinarians are pandemic in the shedrow. Some work for trainers, others for the track. Private vets try to keep the horses running—by injection, heat, or rest. Painkillers are remorselessly overprescribed, permitting unsound horses to race. They don't feel their pain, until they snap a leg off. Track vets aim more for propriety. They keep lists of horses too unsound to race, examine questionable starters in the stable and at the gate. They're protecting the bettors and the track. Sometimes they even protect the horses.

The horse in this picture has broken down during a workout. Mornings are the most dangerous times; everybody's so relaxed. More horses and riders get killed during workouts than during races. It happens easily, requires only a misstep. The exercise boy dismounts, holds the horse, removes the tack, stands straight, tries to swallow.

The vet feels for damage. It's in the ankle, no good sign at all. The horse van, drawn by a tractor, approaches from the rear, like some ominous Wagnerian insect, some harbinger of a motorized afterlife. The rest of the scene remains idyllic, as in a fairytale. The horse's stablemate looks on quietly. Everybody else tries not to notice, knowing doom when they see it.

MORNING BREAKDOWN *Monmouth Park, 1986*

Auction

It's possible to parlay a Cleveland State diploma into a corner office on Wall Street; it's just *more* possible if you did some time at Harvard. Certain prophecies *always* fulfill themselves.

It's also possible to win the Kentucky Derby with a half-breed (out of Mexico, by Truck, as the bluegrass witticism has it). But you boost your chances significantly by shopping uptown for the bloodlines. If anatomy is destiny, breeding is predestination.

Not that paying top dollar guarantees you a runner. It just gives you an edge, and a cushion. An aristocratic yearling who can't outrun a fat man can still be used for breeding. Like the unemployable Harvard man, he need never be unemployed.

This is the part most bettors never see. It begins in the breeding shed and will continue at the training farm. In between, a lot of interests press the flesh.

In recent years, breeding economics have eclipsed racing economics. New money has transformed the market. Arab money. Japanese money. Shopping-Mall-Magnate-With-Matching-Tie-And-Hankie money. Prices have skyrocketed—$13,100,000 for a Nijinsky colt; $40,000,000 for Shareef Dancer in syndication. Racing purses have grown almost irrelevant. Stakes' winners retire early, dodging injury. Potential has taken precedence over accomplishment.

The best yearlings, and the worst, stay with their breeders. The worst can't be sold; the best won't be. The in-betweens go to the block. Some turn out to be champions. The choicest are sold at Keeneland and Saratoga. Breeding stables sell them to racing stables. Auction houses do the middling, for five percent.

The horse in this picture is one year old. It's been living out back the past week, in a stall decked out like Laura Ashley's mausoleum. It's been combed and curried, polished and primed, scouted obsessively by prospective bidders. Tonight's the night.

They stay in their stalls until their numbers come up. Ash-blond window shoppers saunter discreetly down their rows. Ancient grooms nod knowingly from antique camp chairs. The auctioneer's voice drifts down from the pavilion. The moon provides some light, colored lanterns more. A summer breeze rustles the dark trees. Preemptive laughter and the click of ice cubes complement the mix. The self-consciousness of it all only heightens the effect.

They're led into the ring by hip number. One white-jacketed groom leads. Another follows, sweeping up their indiscretions. The auctioneer recites their lineage. It's all described in the catalogue, but sellers like to sell. The caller must be discreet, though, play the headmaster soliciting handouts during matins.

Bids are made. Bids are insulted. Higher bids are called for. Each plateau is labeled a giveaway. Finally the gavel falls, a deal is struck. The yearling returns to its stall. It will go to its new owners tomorrow. The biggest moment of its career may have passed.

The black-tuxedoed men, standing, are bid spotters. The dowdy frocks and half glasses belong to the old money. The balcony dwellers, above the bidboard, are the "nontraditional" interests, a Social Register euphemism for rag traders and gum chewers. Outside the pavilion, their noses pressed to the plate glass, stand the real nontraditional interests, the everyday race-trackers. They huddle there all night, five deep, annotating their catalogues, estimating bids, imagining themselves Whitneys for an evening.

It's a curious paradox, this reverence for blue blood among working stiffs. The auction ring seems to bring out their true yearnings, much as royal weddings elicit the latent Tory in London charwomen.

YEARLING SALE *Saratoga Race Course, 1979*

Tip Sheet

RESOLVING UNCERTAINTY is the handicapper's goal. Resolving it unaided is his fantasy. It makes him feel momentarily omniscient, as if any confusion might eventually bend to his will.

In fact, the scientific horseplayer, impervious to whim, does not exist. Fact and opinion blend seamlessly at the track. The odds board is a fact, its conclusions just a collective guess in numbers.

For the chronically weak-willed, there's no shortage of advice at the track. It's the home of the unsolicited exhortation. Local papers list picks. The *Racing Form* features eight experts' selections. Factor-in the ubiquitous public buzz, and the judgmental roar soon becomes deafening.

My own preference is to make a preliminary choice, then compare it to the selections of others; affirming my judgment, or undermining it. Either will do.

It's like asking a friend's opinion of your date. It shouldn't matter, but it will.

This man makes his living probing uncertainty, cultivating the public's blind obeisance to expertise, no matter how implausible.

He'll sell you a list of winners for a dollar. He stands outside racetrack gates, chanting unlikely claims, buttonholing the un-wary, calling them "sweetheart," "pal," thrusting his cards into hesitant palms, trading on his presumptuous cordiality. Yesterday's successful selections, adorning his hat, could have been printed sometime this morning.

There were once armies of such men outside every track: Maryland George, Clocker Walker, Lucky Baldwin, with their "Getaway Specials," their "Stable Tips," their "Winner If Wets." Few survive. They've gone the way of the chautauqua ballyhooer, victims of their own colorful improbability.

Who still buys such canned prognostications? Beginners. Nostalgics. The superstitious. Obsessive collectors of opinion. Those for whom rented certainty always tops indigenous hope.

I've never bought one myself. Absolute confidence only *reaffirms* my doubts. Besides, no man can pick winners better than I can; at least not today. And if he could, he wouldn't be selling them for a dollar, or wearing wraparound sunglasses and Big-Band-Sound sideburns.

No, I've never bought such a card, and probably never will. But if I happen to see another bettor holding one, I'll sneak a peek.

MARYLAND GEORGE *Northampton Fair, 1985*

Numbers*

LARGEST STRAIGHT-WAGER PAYOFF at a North American track: $1885.50, $644.60, $172.60, paid by Wishing Ring at Latonia, June 17, 1912. (I had it, incidentally. It figured.)

Largest multi-wager payoff at a North American track: $1,132,466, to one bettor for a pick-six ticket at Bay Meadows, December 13, 1985. (In most states, payoffs are rounded to the nearest twenty cents *below* the actual price. Thus horses that should pay $9.87 actually pay $9.80. The extra seven cents, called breakage, goes to the state.)

Average takeout per track: seventeen percent, of which eight percent typically goes to the state, six percent to the track itself, and three percent to the horsemen in the form of purses. (The house edge in blackjack is one percent.)

Number of racetracks in North America: eighty-nine.

Total amount wagered last year: $8,254,612,623.

Largest handle last year: Santa Anita, $691,864,682 for 121 days, an average of $5,717,889 per day.

Smallest handle last year: Harbor Park, $183,687 for six days, an average of $30,614 per day.

Total racetrack attendance last year: 54,998,805.

Highest average purse per race: $33,319, at Saratoga.

Lowest average purse per race: $500, at Harbor Park.

Leading money-winning horse of all time: John Henry, $6,597,947.

Amount it costs to keep the average horse in training at a top track: $55 per day.

How purses are divided: sixty percent to the winner, twenty percent for second, ten percent for third, six percent for fourth, two percent for fifth.

Trainers fees: all expenses, plus ten percent of purses won.

Most money won by a jockey in a year: $13,415,049, by Laffitt Pincay, Jr., in 1985.

Most races won by a jockey in a year: 546, by Chris McCarron in 1974.

Most money won by a jockey, all time: $106,054,127, by Laffitt Pincay, Jr., in twenty years of riding.

Most races won by a jockey, all time: 8,507, by Bill Shoemaker, from 38,145 mounts, in thirty-seven years of riding.

Most races won in one day by a jockey: eight, in ten mounts—by David Gall, at Cahokia Downs, October 18, 1978; by Chris Loseth, at Exhibition Park, April 9, 1984; and by Robert D. Williams, at Lincoln, September 29, 1984.

Jockeys fees: Ten percent of purse for win, five percent for place or show, forty to a hundred dollars for unplaced mounts, depending on the value of the race and the track.

Most races won by a trainer in a year: 496, by Jack Van Berg in 1976.

Most races won by an owner in a year: 494, by Dan Lasater in 1974.

Highest priced yearling of all time: Seattle Dancer, a colt by Nijinsky II out of My Charmer, bought by Robert Sangster and partners for $13.1 million on July 23, 1985, Keeneland, Kentucky.

Highest priced horse of all time: Shareef Dancer, $40 million for forty syndicated shares at $1 million apiece, paid to Sheikh Mohammed Bin Rahid al Maktoum.

Highest stud fee of all time: Northern Dancer, $1 million.

Horse with best win-loss record: Kinesem, 54 for 54 (1876–79).

Most winners picked in one day by a public handicapper: ten on a ten-race card, by Charles Lamb of the *Baltimore News American* at Delaware Park, July 28, 1974.

Entry fees for a typical $200,000 stakes race: $200 to nominate, $2,000 to pass the entry box, $2,000 to start.

Entry fee for the average race: $0.

Admission to Belmont Park: five dollars for the clubhouse, two dollars for the grandstand.

Minimum bet when I started going to the track: two dollars.

Minimum bet now: one dollar.

*Statistics as of 1987

MAKING CHANGE *Keeneland, 1985*

Race Day

THOROUGHBREDS LIKE TO RACE. It's their job. They're bred for speed, and need to use it. Horses in training must compete regularly. They'll pace in their stalls if they don't; they'll kick the walls down.

Racehorses always know when it's time. They read it in various eyes, smell it in the air, sense it in the activity around them. They know today's the day.

They wake at the usual hour, but something's different, something's off. They're not fed as much. They don't go to the track. They're just walked a bit, checked by the vet, returned to their stalls—to wait. All morning they're deferred to, chatted up, paid attention, as on a birthday.

By afternoon the backstretch is empty. The chores are done. Everybody's gone racing. A lone groom sits by a stall, listening to the radio, watching the clock. He's talking to his horse, as to a child, or to himself. The horse has his front legs in a bucket; they're being "iced," to numb the soreness. The two are alone, edgy, yet equable, in an anticipatory trance.

The call comes abruptly on the intercom: "Bring them up for the sixth race." It's anticipated, yet unexpected. The groom jumps up, turns off the radio, crushes his cigarette. He fastens a shank to the bridle, removes the feet from the bucket, opens the stall door. Off they go, as simple as that.

They walk past their neighbors, along the dirt path. They're waved at, wished luck. These are competitors, but sympathizers, made confederates by the horses. They navigate the entire backstretch, the deserted village, up one street, down another, around a corner, across a lawn.

At the end of the path lies the track. They enter it, see the grandstand in the distance, the crowd gathered to it. Everything seems so small from here, so inconsequential. To the groom it seems momentarily irrelevant, and distinctly foreign, to their backstretch life, to life in general. It's like a drive-in theatre viewed across a lake.

They walk along, sinking into the track; it's like sand. Other horses join them—the competition. Some hurry, others lag. They form a line of sorts. Horses from the previous race walk toward them, returning to their barns. Their nostrils flare, their veins bulge, they dance on tip-toe, straining against their handlers.

The stands draw nearer. Some bettors hug the rail, staring dumbly, consulting programs. A few pass remarks. No attention is paid. The horses sense it now. It's coming closer. First-timers fidget; some even buck. Veterans prick up their ears. The transition is almost made. They can see the paddock now, the owners, trainers, factotums, the bulk of the crowd. They can make out the entire apparatus. They keep moving toward it, giving themselves over, becoming part of it, losing the other part.

This picture portrays the midpoint of the trip. Four racehorses. Four ponies. An appropriate number of grooms and pedestrians. It would be about the sixth race, judging from the litter. Ten percent of the crowd lines the rail, about standard.

BRINGING THEM UP *Keeneland, 1985*

42

Program

It costs fifty cents now, stands nine inches, has twenty pages.

It's full of useless and self-aggrandizing information: names of track officials, directions to the souvenir stands, neutron-bomb evacuation procedures, instructions on placing bets (though not, alas, on how to win them).

It offers some worthwhile intelligence as well: jockey and trainer standings, post-position statistics, where to pick up your absolutely free souvenir painter's cap, and, of course, its raison d'être, today's racing menu.

Each race gets its own page, and often, these days, its own name. If your luck is changing, this name is Le Prix de l'Arc de Triomphe. If it's holding, it's the Bayonne Junior Kiwanis Handicap.

Each event is described by distance, surface, purse, and condition. Races have eligibility requirements. Some are just for fillies, others strictly for two-year-olds. Many are for horses who've won seldom, or earned little. Races are "written" by the racing secretary, whose job it is to draw large, competitive fields. It's the trainer's job to find underpopulated, soft ones.

Each runner is listed by number, along with its name and a violently abbreviated biography. The basics are owner, trainer, jockey, parents, sex, age, and earnings. The embellishments are color, probable odds, weight assignment, silk tones. Equipment changes are listed at the end, along with the scratches. Scratched horses have had their regrets accepted regretfully, due to track condition, illness, or whim.

Handicapping selections used to be offered for every race. This practice has been widely discontinued.

The program is the racetrack equivalent of *Playbill*—the scorecard we can't tell the players without. It's necessary, and even more, it's endemic. It proves we're back.

Here's what we do with our programs:

We buy one on entering the track, from our lucky vendor in his pulpit-like kiosk. He's always serving six customers at once, pushing quarters around like jumbo Parcheesi disks. We look to see if the cover has been changed. It hasn't—it's still the smiling horseshoe cradling the out-of-register jockette. We scan it avidly for rider changes, to see if our hot horse is still in. We pencil in late revisions, taking the track announcer's dictation, or cribbing from the blackboard out back. We write little reminders to ourselves, circle jockeys' names, transcribe overweights. We pull it in and out of our pockets obsessively, checking facts, reaffirming hunches. We record results after every race, or intend to, but get distracted, and don't. We drop it as we're walking to the paddock and some fat guy with hair in his ears yells, "Hey buddy, you dropped your program." We lose it and have to buy another. We read it on the subway going home and notice things we should have noticed earlier. We save it for months, or years, or forever. We hold it all afternoon, prayerfully, for reassurance.

BEFORE THE DOUBLE *Great Barrington Fair, 1978*

Names

DRUMTOP. Hitting Away. Beat the Traffic.

Naming a racehorse is no casual matter. There are rules. All names must be approved by the Jockey Club. You can't use the name of a living person without permission, or a famous horse's name, or any name used in the past seventeen years. You can't advertise, or politic, or cuss. You're allowed just eighteen characters, including spaces. Numbers must be spelled out. You can't change a horse's name after its first start. Before that, each change will cost you a hundred.

Every season, 40,000 new thoroughbreds are registered. They are named in a predictable variety of fashions—arbitrarily (after a girlfriend or a shopping mall), by rote (combining the father's first name with the mother's second), or as they should be (extrapolating from their lineage some sly poetic reference). Good horses tend to have evocative names. Bad horses tend to have cheesy names. The fish rots from the head.

On a recent afternoon, the following horses ran at Saratoga: Shadowmar, Cullindale, Country Pleasures, Cognizant, Beveled, Cost Conscious. The same afternoon, these horses ran at the Marshfield Fair: Pan Yan, Pet the Jet, Winlocs Raymond, Tarzano, Sparkling Bid, Doctor Beth.

Reflective owners choose lyrical names, full of wry allusions and romantic misdirection. Unimaginative owners prefer cute names, heavy with cloying rhymes and prolish possessives. Some other names from Saratoga: Dance Mask, Temperate, Wench, Twas Ever Thus, LeSauteur, Musical Lark. From Marshfield: Awp's Superman, Little Jello, Sweet a Muffin, Chrissy Baby, K.C.'s Treasure, Paul's Cha Cha, Trash Can.

The derivations of the seemly names are evident: Cognizant (by Explodent out of I Understand); Beveled (by Sharpen Up out of Sans Arc); Cost Conscious (by Believe It out of Penny Gown), Twas Ever Thus (by Olden Times out of Popularity Plus). The punk names betray no correlations. They seem to have been chosen arbitrarily, or by the owner's mistress, as real-estate developers name their subdivisions: Drunken Jack (by King Nashua out of Circle Serenade), Guitar Boogie (by Corn off the Cob out of Run Selma Run), Butch's Folly (by King Jerry out of San Shel).

Great horses, appropriately named, seem even greater: Sword Dancer, No Robbery, Youth, All Along, Running Comment, Allez France, Stir the Embers. Great horses with gauche names seem somehow devalued: Seattle Slew, Spectacular Bid, Trinycarol, Fran's Valentine, Mom's Command.

Many bettors pick their horses by name, though few admit it. Hardened handicappers disdain such sentimentality, then rationalize horses whose names have seduced them, names that mean more to them than they really want them to. It's just another case of illusion following need; of emotional revisionism. It's what permits parents to believe their children are intelligent.

Who remembers the annual Kentucky Club yearling contest?

You had to name an expensive foal, then submit your entry before Derby day. The best name won the yearling. Judge's decision final. Actually, the winning names were always pretty prosaic, but I thought they shouldn't be, and kept entering.

The year I was sixteen I knew I had it nailed. The yearling was by Eastern Flight out of Greek Queen. I called it Icarus. Icarus escaped from Crete on wings fashioned by Daedelus, his father. In his rapture the boy flew too near the sun, his wings melted, and he fell into the sea, and drowned.

The horse was won by a housewife from Daytona Beach, Florida, who named it Eastward Ho.

I haven't entered the contest since. Perhaps they don't hold it anymore. I still fantasize about naming my own yearling though, sometime, somehow. When my time comes I intend to be ready. Here, though no one has asked, is my current short list: L'enfant du Paradis (after the French movie), Blau Reiter (after the German painting school), Easter Week (after the Irish punch-up), Ambivalence (after my favorite racetrack emotion).

GROOM WITH HORSES *Marshfield Fair, 1978*

Invisible

SOME THINGS just aren't there anymore.

Bookies once ran the track—vivacious sports in straw boaters and plaid four-in-hands, scribbling odds changes on portable chalkboards. They live on in England, and in memory. The totalizator has obliterated them here.

Races used to start behind tapes. Now they use electronic gates.

Buglers once blew the call to post. Tape recorders have replaced them at most tracks. At some, it's no longer done at all.

Cameras have made placing judges superfluous. Electronic beams parallel the finish line; the first horse across it breaks the plane.

Scores of racetracks have disappeared: Havre de Grace, Kenilworth, Narragansett—leveled for parking lots, converted to dog racing. The old Jamaica track still has a subway stop, but no track.

The ambiance of the old tracks is waning, sacrificed to the beer-cooler slobs. Hialeah threatens to vanish every year.

Horses evaporate inscrutably. They retire without warning, leaving no trace—unless they're famous, in which case they depart more conspicuously. But they're still gone. Jockeys open video arcades. Trainers go into real estate.

Other things remain, but remain invisible.

The backstretch is invisible to most bettors, like backstage at *Lohengrin*. The track's offices are buried inside the plant, cleverly camouflaged, permanently off-limits. We never see the stewards, the racing secretary, the guys in suits. Can we be certain they exist?

A few things are there to be seen, yet defy perception: the concessionaires, the Pinkertons, the outriders. Pony boys lead the horses to the track, curbing the feisty ones, as their ponies calm the anxious. They work free-lance, fifteen dollars per race. They're always there, but we look right through them. They're like bridesmaids, or toll takers. The track wouldn't be the same without them, but we wouldn't know it if they left.

These two are partners. You can tell. Each pony boy has one pony; none are thoroughbreds. They're placid animals, malleable and competent, like their masters. Next to the thoroughbred they seem as prosaic as appliances.

These two await their next assignment, inside a dingy intratrack passageway. They stare evenly at the camera, flaunting their inconspicuousness, indifferent to our indifference to them; resigned, even gratified, to be invisible.

PONY BOY *Santa Anita Park, 1986*

Agent

AGENTS ARE EASY TARGETS. They deserve to be. They're function is basically parasitical, and they never return a call. They don't mind being hated, though; it's their perk.

Of course they're necessary. The talent would work for nothing without them, or never work at all. Agents' personalities preclude this. They have more enthusiasm for their clients than their clients do. They thrive on rejection. And they're not only capable of facing the world, they seem to want to.

Jockey agents deviate slightly from this norm. They shun Armani suits, rarely lunch at Lutèce. It's the racetrack's bonhomie they're really attracted to: the intrigue, the kinship, the grunge. Moolah runs a distant second, though it's all they ever talk about. They bury their romanticism in clouds of Runyonesque banter. No serious con seeks his fortune peddling jocks.

Most agents are small-timers, trainers temporarily between owners, retired Buick salesmen with fantasies of the fast lane. They take the books of a few marginal riders, then try to squeeze a marginal living from them.

Big-time agents need only one rider. A top jockey can make $1,000,000 a year. His agent takes twenty-five percent. Figure it out. The agent has.

Small-time agents spend most of their time hustling, trying to get their clients on live horses, or, barring that, on any horse. Improbable horses sometimes win. Riders need to win to ride. Conversely, they must ride to win. It's the standard double-bind, racetrack style.

So the agents scurry from barn to barn before dawn, lobbying trainers, cajoling owners, begging for a shot. They call in favors, exaggerate acquaintanceships, make like Broadway Danny Rose without the bird act.

"My new kid handles the stick like McCarron, Pancho," they tell trainers. "He fit that filly you got in tomorrow just poifect."

Big-time agents do little selling; they've got the goods. Their function is largely advisory, and political. They pick the best horses for their protégés, then try to keep spurned trainers as clients. They're all superb handicappers, too, and accomplished snoops. They're not above swapping confidences for consideration.

Every agent is a father to his boy, keeping him sober, watching his weight, building his confidence. It's a charming Dickensian liaison: the big men with the bluff and the pinky rings, the little guys in their faded silk monkey suits. You see them huddled in odd corners of the backstretch, miniaturized Fagins consulting edgy Artful Dodgers. No wonder agents come to confuse themselves with their charges.

"I'm riding Barrera's colt in the feature," they tell acquaintances. "And I think I got a hell of a shot."

In an ideal world, everyone would have an agent—to negotiate washroom privileges, to ask dark strangers for dates. Naturally, only those who don't need agents have them. Successful jockeys could book their own mounts, had they the time.

The jockey in this photograph is the superb Panamanian, Jorge Velasquez. He appears fuzzily disembodied for the moment, as if shocked to discover himself in such circumstances. He's letting his agent be him for these purposes. We're not certain the other gentleman *is* his agent, or anyone's agent for that matter. But if he isn't, he's wasting a world of gestalt. He seems both wary and avidly mercantile. He has a gift for making seersucker look like sharkskin. His way with a panatela is beyond reproach. He has no neck.

He fits it poifect.

BEFORE THE RACE *Saratoga Race Course, 1981*

Tips

Tips are everywhere at the track. They're part of the wallpaper. They don't succeed more often than other bets. They just seem to, because they're juicier. It's impossible to tell a good tip from a bad one; neither precedence nor source are a guide. By the time you hear even the best tip it's too late, of course. Everybody else has already heard it, and killed the odds. That's a constant with tips—no matter who you are, you're always the last to know.

All horseplayers tip occasionally, claiming inside knowledge, whether they have it or not. It's an ego boost for the tipper, just another source of confusion for the tippee. Other than that, tips do little damage, unless they come from touts.

The word *tout* comes from the Anglo-Saxon *totian*, meaning "to peep." To tout originally meant to spy on horses in training, to learn which were fastest. It later came to mean the selling of such information to gamblers. Finally, it came to mean those who did the selling.

Newcomers to the racetrack fear touts disproportionately, as visitors to Manhattan dread muggers. They're a metaphorical focus for all their horror. Newcomers think every other bettor is a tout. In fact, every other bettor just *looks* like a tout.

The Warner Brothers image of the tout persists charmingly, the weasel-faced sharpie in the snap-brim fedora. Actually, touts only survive by not looking like touts, and by seducing those who can't tell the difference.

Clubhouse touts are the smoothest. Few use the term *psssssst* to introduce themselves. Fewer still are named "Pee Wee" or "Dutch." Perpetually tanned, aggressively manicured, they table-hop like Vatican envoys on speed, flashing ivories, showing cuff.

They're virtually indistinguishable from the big shots they bamboozle. That's the idea. They don't give out many horses. They know selectivity nurtures recidivism in their clients. They never seem to suffer from being wrong, either. Their charm makes all inaccuracies seem beside the point.

Grandstand touts are more folksily nondescript, the better to match the pedestrianism of their marks. They wear J. C. Penney windbreakers and smoke Tiparillos. They seem so friendly, so regular-like. They could be neighbors. Their stories go something like this: A trainer gave them a cinch tip in the next race, but their wallet's been stolen. If you buy them a ticket they'll tell you the horse's name. A surprising number of sane people go for this. The usual percentage win. The tout returns to *them* for the real payoff.

What people fear in the tout also seduces them: the notion that somebody knows, and that somebody isn't them. The tout claims special knowledge, like all shamans. In an anarchic environment, he promises control. Marks doubt he can deliver. But what if he can? It's not weakness touts prey on, but the fear of being weak. Marks risk betrayal not to be excluded.

So the tips proliferate—the hot stories, the inside dope—perpetuating the soothing myth of expertise. It's a punk bargain, freely entered into, the will to believe.

The men in this picture aren't touts; they're just garden-variety railbirds. But they're what people believe touts should look like. It makes you wonder. Do these guys look like they know anything we don't? But, armed with the proper con, couldn't they, and wouldn't they, just?

RAILBIRDS *Santa Anita Park, 1986 .*

Telegraph

"THE TRUE ART OF FICTION," Hemingway called it.

Possession of one legitimizes the horseplayer, to himself, to his cohorts. To be without one is to feel like a tourist.

It comes in three editions: eastern, midwestern, and western. The eastern edition is full sized. The others are tabloids—their statistics are less detailed. They throw eastern gamblers for a loop. "Am I supposed to handicap with this little thing? What did they do with the rest of it?"

In the East, it used to be called the *Morning Telegraph*, or "the Telegraph," or "the Telly." Many horseplayers still call it this, and take those who do likewise more seriously.

It's the journal of record for the racing community; *the* source of enlightenment for the handicapper.

It's printed every day, 365 days a year, in Hightstown, New Jersey. At four dollars, it's the world's costliest daily paper. Its price increases are how we track inflation.

Where you buy it makes a difference. It's best bought at a corner store run by a guy with masking tape on his glasses. A good alternative is an outdoor kiosk whose proprietor calls you pal. "The *Racing Form*? Sure, pal, right over there."

You should buy it the night before, to sleep on it. Rising at dawn to trudge through empty streets is a viable option. Just don't wait too long; it often sells out early. You can find yourself in some very vivid neighborhoods hunting up a *Form*.

My father used to buy it at South Station in Boston late Friday night. We would stand in the vast, empty terminal waiting for the "paper train" to arrive from New York City. Curtains of steam would roll across the darkened platforms. Small knots of silent handicappers attended our vigil.

Waiting for the *Form* is a pleasant ritual, any time, any place.

It's a timeless constant, a chance to talk. Often, it's the best part of the racing day.

Many people buy it at the track. Standing in line to slip one from the stacks is reassuring; it reminds you that you're back.

Some bettors open its pages instantly, right there, right next to the vendor. They desperately need to check some fact, or reaffirm some inkling. Others discard everything but the past performances, the nonliterati.

In the 1920s, there were too many turf sheets to count. Moe Annenberg, the race-wire baron, owned the biggest. John D. Hertz, the rental-car magnate, funded the runner-up. Moe bought out John, then did a stretch in Lewisburg for tax evasion. The Annenberg publishing empire, now run by Moe's son Walter, eventually included the *Philadelphia Enquirer* and *TV Guide*. But the *Racing Form* has always been its cornerstone.

Look at the *Form* in this photograph. It always looks, and reads, exactly like this. The headline might say, "Alomas Ruler Faces Seven on Hollywood Turf," but it's always about the day's top race, and always scans like an editorial in *Variety*.

The rest of the paper is equally invariable. Feature-race previews fill the front page, chatty local columns ("Turf Topics") adorn the back. They read like computerized solicitation letters, or canned spring-training stories. Only the names and dates ever change.

The *Racing Form* doesn't criticize, or editorialize, or investigate. It just reports, accentuating the positive. It doesn't have to do anything any differently. It's the Bible.

It carries exactly two nonracing features: a brief news summary from Reuters, and Barney Nagler's sports column. It used to run theatre reviews, but somebody noticed.

BETTOR AT THE RAIL *Laurel Race Course, 1985*

Everything else in it concerns racing: entries and results from all American tracks, charts from the major ones, workouts, expert selections, equine cartoons, ads for sires, linament endorsements. It says no other world exists.

Two features are invaluable, if little read—the foreign racing pieces, written with a 1930s continental panache, and the breeding column, "Bloodlines," composed as though all the world was chromosomes. To peruse these is to take a holiday from provincialism, to expand one's world beyond the bald practicalities of the moment.

The most intriguing reading is always "Official Rulings." It reports which jockeys have been fined for "altercations," which grooms were caught smoking under the shedrow, which trainers have been suspended for hanging paper. It's like the police-blotter column in a weekly suburban newspaper.

"Oaklawn. Pony girl Tracy Stander, S.S. No. 639–24–7382, D.O.B. 9/7/52, is hereby fined $25 for conduct unbecoming a pony girl on Monday, April 11, 1987."

Conduct unbecoming a pony girl?

Still, the *sine qua non* of the *Form* is the past-performance records. Each runner has its last ten tries annotated, in finite detail. There is no more comprehensive chronicling in sport.

The *Form* is *the* symbol. It brings it all back, as sand pails evoke the seashore. The past-performance records are the symbol's text. We're looking for the key, the oracular detail. Life resists such efforts, so we're trying it with horses.

Hemingway was right.

RACING FORM VENDOR *Great Barrington Fair, 1978*

Commentary

IF YOU ARRIVE LATE you can't find a *Racing Form*. They've stopped selling them; they've gone home to Queens. It's a disaster.

The serious horseplayer, deprived of his *Form*, is like Magellan without his maps. It's not that he can't pick a winner, it's that he can't pick one *right*, can't *figure* it.

A *Form* must be found, then, even if it means fishing one from the trash. Which is *exactly* what it means.

Abandoned *Racing Forms*, like Mayan pottery shards, conjure up the ghosts of former owners. Some are found folded on grandstand chairs, a bit too neatly. Others are discovered crumpled in "receptacles," hurled there in sudden relapses of despondency.

Handwritten annotations often cover them, the personal testaments of their abandoners. Every horseplayer has his own hieroglyphics: scribbled formulas, arrows to toyland. Discovering a stranger's makes one feel a trifle queasy. It's like overhearing a grown man saying his prayers.

Professional commentary is much less personal, yet equally obique. Public handicappers crank out their cryptic assessments, like those this man is trying to decipher. Favorites get hedged guarantees: "never better," "likely repeater," "class here." Contenders receive qualified endorsements: "needed last," "just missed," "another chance." Inscrutable horses have their inconsistencies codified: "best needed," "drops weight," "smart barn." Even horror horses are thrown a verbal bone: "been tiring," "must improve," "in tough today."

Certain tags elicit negative empathy: "long overdue," "been disappointing," "best, poor lot." Others we'd welcome seeing on our tombstones: "always there," "can't eliminate," "fast, fit, dangerous."

We think they're gospel, because they're printed, and they're terse. They seem irrefutable even after they've been discredited.

The noblest commentary, however, adorns the daily charts.

"Our Elise made the pace under clever handling, maintained a clear advantage into the stretch, then responded with good courage to turn back After Midnight. The latter, reserved early, loomed boldly at the eighth pole, but wasn't good enough. Up Anchor, forwardly placed, made a brief bid on the far turn, but weakened under pressure, and failed to menace."

The prose is always this precisely evocative—latinate clauses full of vivid, martial imagery. They're miniature novels, really; Walter Scott plots with Jane Austen diction; narrative proof that horses' characters are their fates.

The comments we live by, however, are those on the past-performance pages. These used to be quite lively. Now they're dismissively generic. Winners win either "easily," or "handily," or "driving." Runners-up are always "game," or "sharp," or "second best." Quitters "tire," or "weaken," or "give way." Mid-pack finishers "rally," or "fade," or run "evenly."

Such nebulousness makes us long for past explicitness, for the commentary that justified our blind faith in it. We grow nostalgic for the dismal efforts labelled "dismal efforts," for the sore horse all could see "came back lame," for the front-runners who stole the lead and were "never headed," for the bold finishers who closed to win it "going away."

CHECKING THE FORM *Santa Anita Park, 1986*

Handicapping

ACCORDING TO ANDREW BEYER, the *Washington Post's* esteemed handicapper, "If you have one chink in your psychological armor, playing the horses will bring it out in an instant."

One chink?

If?

Exposing every weakness is the purpose of the exercise. Life is a metaphor for the track.

Nowhere are our shortcomings more obvious than in our handicapping. Thousands of factors vie for relevance; which we emphasize tells us who we are.

Everybody agrees on the three important variables. Class. Form. Speed. Nobody agrees on their order.

Secondary factors are legion. Some handicappers worry about all of them; others specialize. Among the major ones are age, breeding, consistency, distance, earnings, gender, post position, surface, and weight. There are books that dissect them all in numbing detail. Buy one and drown yourself in nuance.

In fact, handicapping isn't a science. Happenstance often prevails. A hole opens up on the rail, a rider gets a fly in his eye, a favorite just isn't in the mood. The most unlikely things happen routinely. A horse who's quit at six furlongs wins at a mile, befuddling the rationalists, fomenting existential quandaries. Handicappers must forget this and forge on. Life is mystery.

Ultimately, it's a matter of preference. Our standards are objective, our applications personal. I like closers, long shots, narrative detail. Others prefer front-runners, favorites, speed figures. The truth doesn't vary, only our perception of it. Hard-core handicappers revere logic, scorn sentimentality. They see no sentimentality in their faith in human reasoning, no fallaciousness in their dependence on the facts.

Sherwood Anderson put it best in *Winesburg, Ohio*:

"It was the truths that made the people grotesques. The old man had quite an elaborate theory concerning the matter. It was his notion that the moment one of the people took one of the truths to himself, called it his truth, and tried to live his life by it, he became a grotesque and the truth he embraced became a falsehood."

HANDICAPPERS BEFORE THE RACE *Laurel Race Course, 1985*

Beginner's Luck

IT'S THRILLING TO INTRODUCE someone to the track, to take them for the first time. You get to *see* again what you've memorized. You get to renew your vows.

They must be the right type, of course, or show promise of being the right type. It's a particular world; it takes specific *seeing*. You can't take just anyone.

Reactions are swift and symptomatic. The imaginative find it interesting, the banal are bored. Deep thinkers get caught right up in it, can't wait for the next revelation. Unlikely prospects are the most rewarding converts— it's like finding a nun who really likes to tango.

It's best not to make it a test of course, a requisite of friendship. But it's hard not to. You're not just presenting the track to them, you're offering yourself. They may hate it. They may be loftily indifferent. They may like it for all the wrong reasons. The margins are narrow.

They always ask the same questions: How much should I bring? What should I wear? Will you show me? You answer breezily, reassuringly. They sound apprehensive, or eager. They want it to go well.

You give them the crash course: the *Form*, betting procedures. You assure them their opinions are welcome, and valid. Then they're on their own. You remain available, keep kibbitzing. But you want them to see it for themselves, to have their own version.

They reveal their quirks immediately. They bet two dollars on a pretty horse to show, or ten dollars on a hopeless horse to win. They keep their hands in their pockets, pleading poverty. You can learn everything you need to know about someone by taking them to the track. But you can never predict.

You know the real mistakes instantly, right after the first race. "That *was* exciting," they say, biting into their second hot dog, "do you always stay until the very last race?"

The attentive imitate your bets initially. After all, you're the one who "knows." If you're winning, they remain faithful, think you a genius. If you're losing, doubts begin to surface. You can almost feel their deference dwindling. By the fifth race they're ready to roll their own. Very tentatively, almost apologetically, they plunge. You feel a slight parental pang then, of loss, and of identification. They're no longer the clinging infants they were just moments ago.

Frequently they win, which can be annoying, especially if you're losing. It makes it seem too easy. Betting is something you must master before you can even do it wrong.

Don't let it get to you. Just grin and go with it. Take it for what it's worth. There *is* such a thing as beginner's luck. Buy into it. Play their horses. Cash their tickets. Every time should be somebody's first time. On days when you're showing the way, it can be yours again.

VETERAN FAN *Santa Anita Park, 1986*

Solitaries

It can be a convivial place, though it needn't be. Its gregariousness tolerates agnostics. There's no pressure to join in.

Many attend the track in groups: informal clusters that meet regularly in the usual place, organizational packs that are ferried in in buses. For these people, the track is no grand passion; it's their social life.

Others come alone.

It's a punishing conflict—this transitory gregariousness, our yearning for company, our need to be alone. The racetrack offers a temporary middle ground; complete seclusion in the midst of frantic crowds.

This man probably goes to the track once a week. It's his chance to vacate, to shed responsibility, to forget what his real life is to him.

He rises early to buy the *Racing Form,* peruses it throughout breakfast, through second cups of coffee. He counts his money, leaves home, walks to the corner, catches the track bus, nods to the regulars. He enters the grandstand, buys a beer, stands during the National Anthem, bets his doubles. He's where he wants to be, in the realer life.

He will keep his nose deep in the *Form* all day, doping them out, searching for angles. He treasures his anonymity, seeks his identity in it. If he meets someone he knows they'll exchange pleasantries, then quickly part. No offense will be taken. It's racetrack etiquette.

All track solitaries have favorite places to stand, to watch races, or study them. They park themselves next to broken water coolers, or in alcoves behind the binocular-renter's stall; anyplace, as long as it's obscure. Few would choose to do time on these particular stairs, but there's always the exception. These are stairs from the back end of any racetrack, any building actually. They're almost invisible, rarely used, cool passages to nowhere in particular. Solitariness on them is almost another presence.

Spend a month alone on the track. A week into it, your perspective starts to revise itself. The track begins to seem like reality, at least as much as reality ever does. It constructs its own pervasive rhythms, the seductive cadences of voluntary solitude. The good thing is that nobody bothers you. The bad thing is that nobody tries. Nothing disturbs the dream.

Soon, casts of characters begin to emerge from the crowd. You begin seeing the same faces over and over, mostly solitary, always male. These are men who've fled to the track for the order it brings, seeking focus, or relief. They pace through the betting ring, eyes averted, or slouch against some wall somewhere, dressed anonymously, chewing pencils, studying the *Form.* They seem intent on mastering some esoteric technique, or creeping up on some provisional wisdom. They *love* this reality, despise the other. They've taken forever off.

ALONE WITH THE *FORM* *Santa Anita Park, 1986*

Betting

Here's how, if you must know.

Figure out how much cash you'll need. Double it. Put it in your pocket. Consider it gone. Put your expense money in another pocket. Keep these accounts separate; they're different things.

Buy your *Racing Form* early, at the usual place. Allow four hours for study, minimum. Pick a quiet spot. Make yourself a cup of something. Review the races in order. Begin by eliminating impossible horses. One wins occasionally, but it's a start. Rank the survivors in order of preference, in case your choice is scratched, or is overbet. Leave a tough race, go on to the next. When you return, things will look clearer. Eventually it will come down to two horses, or three. Anybody can get it down to three. Don't drive yourself crazy choosing between them, unless you want to. Don't exhaust yourself before the day begins.

Get to the track half an hour early. Avoid public transportation; how you get there sets the tone. Taxis are nice, walking better. Horseback is ideal, but impractical. Wear something jaunty, but not precious. Bring binoculars, and use them. Drop a coin in the Salvation Army tambourine. It's good luck. Note the changes, and the track conditions. Take several deep breaths. Get the feel of the day.

Don't bet the double, or exactas, or any other combinations. It's tough enough picking one horse. Plus, the takeouts are for suckers, the complexities cloud your mind. It's also vulgar, gimmicky. Bet classically, one thing at a time. If you do bet exactas, bet consecutive numbers; they come in frequently.

Bet to win. The payoffs are more rewarding. The aggressiveness is its own reward. Place betting is for doubters, show betting for pantywaists. When you play safe, your horses start winning.

Welcome others' insights, but ignore their judgments, especially insiders. Half of them always tout their horses. The other half never do. If they really knew they wouldn't be telling you. Stand on your own.

Stick with your first choice. Don't talk yourself out of a horse. Don't make side bets to cover eventualities. Follow your instincts, if you have any, and know what they are.

When you buy a winning ticket, go back to that window. It couldn't hurt. Be loyal. Don't back off a horse that's won for you, or bet a horse just because it broke your heart.

Find a good place to stand. Sit as little as possible; it makes you logy, passive. Move around. Walk to the paddock. Look at the horses, and the people. You might see something. Look at the trees, and the sky.

Manage your money. Betting isn't the same as handicapping. How much you bet is as important as what you bet it on. Bet more when you're winning; play with their money. Don't try to get even all at once. Be patient. Don't show off, even to yourself. Don't up your bets to up your thrill. Don't try to compensate. You're going to lose in the long run. The more you bet the more you'll lose. Concentrate on picking winners. Let the winning take care of itself.

Don't follow mistakes. Betting days assume their own momentum; mistakes feed on each other. It's like spelling—you take

CAB CALLOWAY *Saratoga Race Course, 1978*

one wrong turn, panic, start guessing, try improbable letters, go crazy. Keep calm. Start again, from scratch.

Don't try to separate several good horses, or pick the best of a terrible lot. There are unbeatable races, unbeatable cards. Skip them. Don't force a bet. Show them who's boss.

Pause occasionally, remember the world, regain perspective. Observe other bettors, imagine them someplace else. Never identify.

Avoid favorites, especially short ones. Certain horses, certain types, are always overbet. Above all else, avoid sure things. "Can't lose" horses *can* lose, and *will* lose. Other than that, ignore the odds. Bet a horse, not a price. It's impossible, but try.

Have an idea, a theme. You're going to bet a certain way; you might as well know what it is.

Do something new. Play a hunch. Talk to a security guard. Make an excursion to the far turn to watch the race from there.

Don't bet off the track, at O.T.B., with bookies, sending bets with friends. It's like drinking in the morning.

Have I forgotten anything?

Probably.

Don't eat until you've had a winner. Don't drink, period.

Don't socialize, unless you've picked your horses.

Don't eliminate a horse because somebody you hate loves it.

Don't fish for omens.

Don't let losing streaks embitter you, or winning streaks carry you away. There's nine more tomorrow.

Don't fall in love with a horse, or a style.

Don't lose yourself in betting, or you're gone.

LOSING BETTORS *Keeneland, 1985*

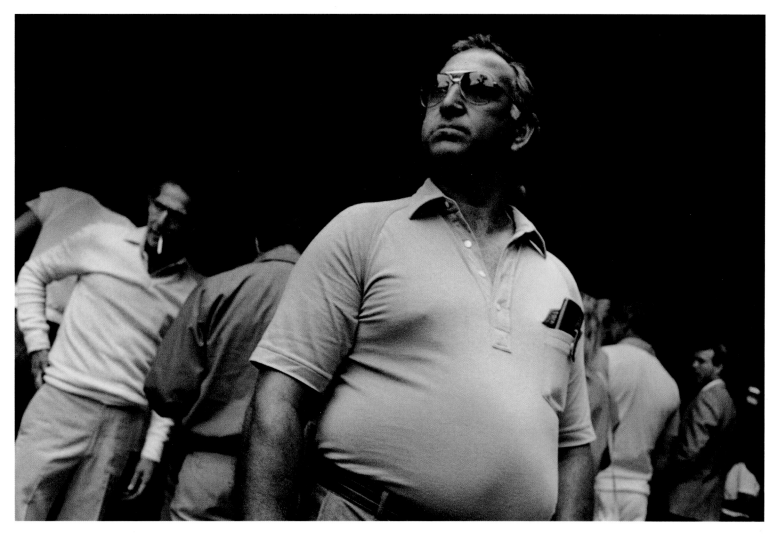

LOSING BETTORS *Saratoga Race Course, 1985*

Identifier

June 3, 1977.

Dr. Mark Gerard, a New York veterinarian, flies to Montevideo, Uruguay, to buy two racehorses. Gerard, forty-three, has built a $250,000-a-year racetrack practice on cortisone shots and stallside charm. He was once Secretariat's vet. He's looking to expand into breeding.

The two horses he buys are curious opposites. Lebon is an undistinguished four-year-old, winless the past twelve months, with $711 in earnings. He costs $1600. Cinzano is a world-class sprinter, a winner of seven of eight this year, a game second to the South American champion Mogambo last time out. He costs $81,000. Both horses are bays with white stars on their foreheads.

Before leaving Montevideo, Gerard turns his entire inventory over by phone. Lebon goes to his former assistant, Jack Morgan, a fringe trainer, for $10,000. Cinzano goes to Joe Taub, a New Jersey millionaire, for $150,000. These are 600 percent and eighty-five percent markups, respectively, for a service that usually brings a ten-percent commission.

The horses are shipped immediately to Gerard's Long Island farm.

Sometime that evening, his first in this country, Cinzano, the expensive horse, fractures his skull in his stall and dies. Nobody knows how. The body is trucked to a dump in Huntington, New York, where it is buried under thousands of tons of garbage. The $150,000 insurance policy on Cinzano is quickly settled, without fuss.

Three months later, on September 23, 1977, Lebon, the cheap horse, makes his second start in the United States. He has trained uninspiringly since June, finished eleventh in his debut two weeks earlier. Today he's moving up in class. It's the last race on a drizzly, prosaic Friday at Belmont.

Lebon never looks back. He wins on the grass at a mile and a quarter by a widening four lengths, paying $116.

Gerard, whom everybody on the racetrack knows, heads straight for the fifty-dollar window in the clubhouse. He has $1300 in win tickets, plus $600 to show. He walks away with $80,000 in cash.

The gag is that it wasn't Cinzano who died. It was Lebon. Gerard collected the insurance money under Cinzano's name, then ran Cinzano under Lebon's name, to cash his bets.

It's a B-movie kind of plot, but it happens. Just never in the big time, and not in recent memory.

It was all a question of identity, really. Who was Lebon? Who was Cinzano? Who was Mark Gerard? And why did he labor so mightily to disguise two horses, then flaunt his own identity so recklessly?

Horses look alike, even to each other. They smell out the distinctions. At the racetrack, identifiers do it. Each racehorse has a number tattooed on its lip. In the paddock, before every race, the identifier matches numbers and names, to keep out the ringers, to ensure the minimal premise.

They didn't have lip tattoos in Uruguay in 1977.

And that's who Mark Gerard was. A guy who'd made it, then risked it on an angle. A racetrack kind of guy.

IDENTIFIER *Northampton Fair, 1985*

Waiting

RACETRACKERS are obsessed with speed. Yet they spend most of their time waiting. It's an insoluble irony—one of millions.

Bettors wait for starts, for odds changes, for official signs. Horsemen wait for soft spots, for healing bones, for the big horse. Everybody waits for a streak—to begin, or end. The racing day lasts from sunup until dusk. The actual racing part takes about twelve minutes. Even long stretches of that are spent waiting, waiting for your horse to get a call.

Some people hate the waiting; it bores them. The half hours between races make them fidgety. They don't know how to handicap, and don't want to learn. They came to the track on a whim, or somebody brought them.

"That was interesting," they say after the first race. "Where's the beer counter?"

These are people who find life in general a bit deliberate, people for whom nothing is happening when nothing is going on.

Racetrackers consider the waiting another palliative, as long as it has set limits. Anticipation is their purest activity; passive time gives their active time its tension. For a real racetracker, waiting isn't an elongation of time, it's a suspension of time, a chance to do nothing without feeling guilty about it; a chance to brood, to fantasize, to get it right. That's why horseplayers like to get their *Racing Forms* early. There's never really enough time to handicap, and every horse looks like the right horse while you're waiting.

Hot jockeys are among those who don't have to wait. They jump off one horse, change silks, jump on another. They don't have time to wait, have nothing to wait for.

Few jockeys are ever that desirable, though. The rest spend most of their time waiting. They sit across from the pool tables, reading overnights, playing hearts. They're fastidiously dressed for the ninth race by the second. They're waiting for their big break, for their real life to begin.

This is the Fairgrounds, Louisiana, mid-winter. Five jockeys display different waiting mechanisms: anxiety, impatience, contemplation, resignation, eagerness. They're caught in the quintessential hiatus, the dead center of that lull between races. It's too late to be lounging around the jockeys' room, too early to be sauntering toward the paddock. So they're standing in some passage in the great inbetween, waiting for their signal to proceed.

JOCKEYS WAITING *Fair Grounds, 1977*

Paddock

THE PADDOCK is the proscenium. It's where the horses are assembled for the race, to be saddled, and inspected. It's the show before the show.

The horses arrive twenty-five minutes before post time. They're identified, to insure they're who they claim to be. Their connections gather in edgy clumps, chitchatting, killing time. The horses are walked in circles, kept limber.

The valets arrive with the equipment. The jockeys enter, stage left. They're greeted by the trainers, then briefed. The owners just stand there, looking superfluous. Then comes the thrilling call: "Put your riders up." Each trainer gives his jockey a leg up. The field parades once around the paddock, then hits the track.

It's like a one-act play with nine performances daily, nine different casts, nine separate readings. We go to see our horse, allegedly—how it looks, how it's acting. It could be an edge. But it isn't. It just confuses things, like all blind dates. No matter what you expected, it's not it. Often you can't justify the discrepancy, so you fall for some other horse entirely, some horse you hadn't even considered. Once you've seen that horse, no other will do. All its faults seem justifiable. It's like physical love.

There are objective standards. A horse needs balanced conformation, an intelligent head, a quick eye. It should have angled pasterns, strong cannon bones, smooth fetlocks. The legs should be well separated and straight. The horse should appear calm, yet engaged; competitive, yet self-contained. None of this mat-

ters, of course. Many malformed horses can run like the wind.

My standards are always objective; I just don't follow them. I'm taken in by odd colors, dramatic markings, quirky mannerisms. I gravitate to enormous horses, tiny horses, horses with attitudes. In the final analysis, it's in the eyes. I like horses that stare at me. I see myself in them.

The human by-play clarifies even less.

Jockeys aren't athletes in the paddock, they're aldermen. They tip their caps, call everybody mister, ma'am, make eye contact. Trainers become branch managers, finessing details, exuding confidence. Owners struggle to look both essential and relaxed, as if they belonged there. The grooms kibbitz among themselves. They alone have no axe to grind. They alone touch the horses without motive.

This picture portrays a typical paddock subplot, the jockey-trainer confab.

The trainer is Johnny Campo, the Fat Man. He could be a character excised from *Guys and Dolls* as improbable.

The jockey is the splendid journeyman Randy Romero.

They've stepped discreetly out of earshot, to outline strategy. Their horse is being walked in the background.

Romero appears earnest and eager, hands on hips, ready to go at 'em. He's saying just enough to stave off inundation.

Campo is laying it on the line, per usual, absent doubt.

Dig on the tie.

PRE-RACE INSTRUCTIONS *Keeneland, 1985*

Class

How AWFULLY, AWFULLY, AWFULLY good to see you.

Horses find their own levels, according to ability. Having an uncle on the Board doesn't help.

The best run in stakes, for fat purses and big prestige. They must pay their way in. Weights are assigned by the authorities. It's like the Ivy League.

Middle-class horses run in allowance races. The competition is less troubling, the rewards sufficient. Weight is determined by past performance. It's like the suburbs.

Ordinary horses run in claimers, permanently on sale. It's like life.

Class enthralls the handicapper. Money remains the preferred differentiation. The best horses run faster for more.

Snobs tend to bet slumming horses, can't imagine them losing. Democrats back upstarts, projecting their own edgy aims. I like up-and-downers, climbers that have failed and are now settling. They reflect dreams of ennoblement enlightened by the facts.

Handicappers don't bet their class alliances. They bet their fantasies, their prejudices, their fears. They bet on who they think gets the money, or who they wish would.

Human class levels are less apparent on the track, but more fixed. Racetrackers like to believe they are classless, like all good Americans. Look again. The boundaries are loosely defined, yet impenetrable. The knots are tight. Every racetrack has a clubhouse and a grandstand. The clubhouse is further stratified into caste niches: Paddock Boxes, Futurity Clubs, Turf Penthouses. The grandstand is just the grandstand. The practical differences are negligible. It's pure symbolism, like first class in an airplane. You pay a lot more to feel a little superior.

In fact, no sport casts its social net wider. Old money runs it. Middle money anchors it. Short money adds the needed color. All think sharing the passion leavens the differences. And it does—for the moment.

Here is a portrait of the equine rich at play, the horsey set in all its gracious opacity. They arouse mixed emotions in everyone but themselves: a little resentment tinged with admiration; a bit of amusement laced with nostalgia.

They, of course, would deny all distinctions, and mean it. Class perceptions grow dimmer at higher altitudes. Money causes amnesia.

The upper classes are ubiquitous at certain tracks, at certain races. You'll more likely find them at Deauville in August, for example, than at Charles Town in February. Even where not present, though, their influence is. They consider racing their purview, as do the poor. Only the middle class find the track déclassé—which is exactly why they call them middle class.

BEFORE THE INTERNATIONAL *Laurel Race Course, 1985*

Shmoozing

EVERY RACE IS A STORY—this next race, the thousands preceding it. Every horse *has* a story, a web of circumstance, a reason why. Old stories meet to form new stories in each contest. Such encounters inspire verbal handicappers to think out loud, to share their insights, to shmooze.

Shmoozing comes in two forms at the track: precursive and postmortive.

Precursive shmoozing focuses on the upcoming race. "This six horse owes me money. How are the Ridans on grass? Martin's colt worked 1:12 at Monmouth. Can you believe they're betting the four?"

Precursive shmoozers harbor no secrets. All their questions are rhetorical. They thrust and parry, second-guess even their own infallible dictates. What's on their hearts is repeatedly on their tongues. This may not be the most efficient way to handicap. But efficiency has never been its object.

Postmortive shmoozing focuses on the previous race. Its goal is more cosmetic than investigatory. It revolves around two alternating themes: "How I Picked That Winner" (and "How Could You Not Have?"), and "Why My Horse, Which Should Have Won, Didn't."

Many shmoozers are retiring in company; talking horses is their lone social grace. Other shmoozers are chronically indecisive; ritual dialogue helps them make up their minds. All shmoozers are seeking human contact. Neutral topics permit men to have discussions.

The guy in the suspenders is no shmoozer. He's totally absorbed in his calculations, oblivious to distraction. The racetrack has asked him a question. He's struggling to answer it in silence.

The woman on the stairs isn't a shmoozer. She's carrying a pocketbook. She's staring into space.

The people seated at ground level aren't shmoozers, either. Shmoozers don't do folding chairs.

The two men in the foreground are the shmoozers here, devotees of the original talking cure.

The bareheaded one is a village explainer, his arm extended in expository outrage, his expression a blend of pique and self-pity. His friend's function is to provide him with agreement. They're about to trade perceptions on the next race, but first they'll finish dissecting the last. Their jockey moved too soon. Their horse went too wide. You can't trust these kid trainers nowadays. They wuz robbed.

TALKING IT OVER *Northampton Fair, 1985*

Systems

CREATIVE BETTORS concoct their own formulas, or think they do. They settle into their prejudices early, and go from there.

Mimics require self-help books.

All handicapping primers have chapters on "spotting the beatable race," offer suggestions for "eliminating unlikely contenders." They don't promise instant wealth; they leave that to the system books.

System books are for incurable true believers, data worshippers, devotees of the quick fix. They're advertised in all the proley penny dreadfuls, back among the truss blurbs and the Florida-swampland come-ons: *Thirty-six Speed Systems for Profit; Big Bucks with New Class-Rating Breakthrough*. All skirt equivocation deftly, and rarely spare the exclamation points. Their graphics make the *Watchtower* look Bauhausian. And they keep on coming at us. New system wrinkles are born daily. Tilt any handicapping factor, and a fresh axiom appears.

Some systems are seductively simple—they're for horseplayers who move their lips when they *think*. Here, in summary, is one called "Yesterday's Odds," from the euphemistically titled *Treasury of American Turf*:

"Add the closing odds for each horse's last two races. Eliminate two-year-olds, horses over eight, maidens, turf races, nonstarters the past thirty days, and horses that finished nine or ten lengths back their last time out. The remaining horse with the lowest total odds is the play."

The logic here is irrefutable. The betting public may be wrong, but it's less likely to be wrong cumulatively.

Some systems gain credibility through obfuscation. This one is from *Winning at the Races: Computer Discoveries in Thoroughbred Handicapping* by William L. Quirin, Ph.D. (Morrow):

"To find an equation that expresses beaten lengths as a function of post position at $1\frac{1}{16}$ mile: linear regression would produce an equation of the form $Y = A + BX$, where Y, the predicated variable, represents beaten lengths, and X, the predicator variable, represents post position. The goal of the linear regression procedure is to determine the proper values for A and B . . ."

Is it me, or is it getting a little warm in here?

System books are written in all imaginable styles, from the comfortingly matter-of-fact to the smarmily evangelical. Their appeal couldn't be clearer. There's little thinking involved, and no responsibility. Once grasped, the system filters all eventualities through it.

Do systems work?

Certainly not.

If you could beat the races, would you tell anyone how?

The nice thing about systems, though, aside from the light lifting they require, is that they all *seem* to work well at first. This produces a false sense of optimism in the bettor, which is still better than no sense of optimism at all. They're like all fresh starts.

The bad thing about systems is that their flaws are, well, systematic. They're built in. System writers bend their theories around their data, and their data is rarely sufficient to begin with.

I once bought a system, I must admit it. Not a system actually—a device. It was called the Kelcocalculator, for reasons I've long since mercifully forgotten. I was enticed by its scientific packaging, its rational premise, its money-back guarantee. It was endorsed by Eddie Arcaro. I forked over fifty bucks for it. It looked like a slide rule with a breakfast nook.

The Kelcocalculator measured various aspects of pace, then codified them. I read the instructions for about an hour. Then I had a glass of root beer, then I had another, then I returned the Kelcocalculator to its box, tucked into its snug styrofoam bunting.

The thing may have worked, for all I know. I'm still not sure exactly why I returned it. Perhaps I didn't want to solve the mystery that badly. Perhaps I didn't want to solve it *that way*. Or maybe (and this seems more likely) I didn't really want to solve it at all.

READING THE PROGRAM *Northampton Fair, 1985*

System Players

ONE THIRD of all betting favorites win, every year, regardless. The percentage occasionally rises at one track, falls at another. The cumulative proportion is invariably one third.

Think about this.

The public chooses favorites. One third win. These are completely unrelated phenomena—popular presentiment, historical validation. Yet at the track they are inextricably linked. It's as if one third of all our dreams came true.

When I discovered this odd connection, many years ago, it tripped a tiny acquisitive lever in my consciousness. I felt as Fleming must have when his cultures came up moldy; not as though I'd found the answer, but as though the answer was now findable. It caused a thrilling leap of faith in my logic. One irrational constant suddenly equaled hundreds, all undiscovered, all awaiting linkage. Handicapping need no longer be an evasive skill, it could be an acquirable science. I'd be a millionaire.

I spent the next five years searching for more constants. I found many, I linked most. I just never found a way to make them profitable.

One third of all favorites *did* win—but they paid an average $5.40 in doing so. The reward was a constant ten-percent loss. None of my other invariables proved more lucrative. Every improvement in my win curve brought a corresponding dip to my payoff slope. I'd discovered a serum for which there was no known disease.

Where I'd gone wrong seems obvious in retrospect. I'd stumbled on that little knowledge that always proves so dangerous.

I was like the science-fair contestant who reinvents the telephone.

I still believe in my theory, though. It's too mathematically vibrant to abandon, too tantalizingly enigmatic to be useless. Hundreds of obscure connections remain untested. Surely one will eventually make me rich.

The system player is the Gyro Gearloose of the pari-mutuel pools. He doesn't believe in chance, reserves all his reverence for numbers. He puts a plastic overlay on the world. His system may be unconscionably simple-minded (permitting only bets on horses with white dots on their forelegs) or needlessly convoluted (spotlighting beaten favorites dropping in turf sprints). The system player doesn't fight it. He never colors outside his lines.

I like systems. I relish control as much as the next man. But I also like handicapping. What good is having control if you can't waive it? So I combine both approaches whenever possible. To label this a mix of art and science may be a bit grandiose. But it's in the ballpark.

Pure system players are easy to spot at the track. They're the ones scribbling cryptic figures all over their *Racing Forms*, the ones with the clipboards and the ear flaps. Handicappers insist that system players take all the fun out of it. And they do—if by "it" you mean the gambling. Which, of course, is never what system players mean. For system players, the "it" is *always* the system.

PUNTERS *Keeneland, 1985*

Lines

THESE MEN are standing in line to bet.

Half-hour intervals separate the races, enough time to make most rational decisions—if rationality got you to the racetrack, which it didn't. So long lines form at the last minute, full of vacillators trying to act decisively.

Handicappers never really decide between two horses, or three, or ten. They just pretend to, or else they'd never bet. Should they risk five dollars, or fifty? To win, or place? On the favorite, or a long shot? Maybe they should pass this race entirely, or wheel the rail horse with the three first-time starters.

Each betting line achieves its own inevitability. You've picked it carefully. It looked shorter, faster, freer of crazies. Now you can study a few more minutes in peace. The four horse has good workouts. The seven's changing riders. Now *that* line's moving faster. Should you switch? Probably not. The two's adding blinkers. The eight's dropping weight. You check the odds board, and the clock. You'll make it. No, you won't. Yes you will.

In the last minute, the shouting begins—at slow clerks, at slow bettors, at those who don't have their GODDAMN MONEY READY. The pace quickens. Suddenly you're there, naming your number, as if you were sure. Is it the one you imagined? Or have you surprised yourself again?

Sometimes you don't get to name *any* number. The bell rings; the machines lock; it's post time. The clerk keeps punching keys, but gets no response, just the soft click of the disconnected battery. The line collapses, passion spent. You begin rooting *against* your choice. You've been shut out.

This picture captures the full range of betting-line emotions.

The man in the dark suit, at left, appears confident of his choice, but not of having enough time to bet it. He's going to start naming names if he doesn't.

The man behind him, in *the* shirt, is fatalistic. They're going to run this race, so he's going to bet it. But without enthusiasm. He wouldn't mind being shut out, to tell you the truth. He could use the money.

The man in the glasses doesn't know what the hell to do. He's looking around for any available clue, squeezing his *Form*, fingering his bankroll. He's caught in the classic betting-line bind— hoping it will move slower to let him bet wisely, hoping it will move faster to let him bet at all.

Tonight, all three will call it a mixed day at the track. They lost a bundle, but the lines were short.

BETTING LINE *Santa Anita Park, 1986*

Odds

THE TRACK DOESNT *want* you to lose. The track doesn't care. It takes its cut regardless. It only cares *how much* you bet.

Pari-mutuel betting was invented by M. Oller, a Parisian *parfumeur* and lottery dabbler. In 1872, Oller began booking bets on French racing. For a while he lost money. Then he devised a system that allowed his customers to bet among themselves and divide the winnings proportionately. Oller called his method *pari-* (from *parier*, "to bet") *mutuel* ("among ourselves"). He opened an office on the Boulevard des Italiens, and got very rich.

Since Oller, racetrackers have been betting against each other. The enemy is us.

We push our dollars through the little windows. They're tallied electronically. A fixed percentage is skimmed, and kept. The rest is returned to winning bettors, in proportions predicted by the odds board.

The odds mesmerize us. They're everywhere—under each staircase, around every corner. We monitor them continuously. They change every ninety seconds, undermining opinions, or confirming them.

Two desires fuel our numeric obsession: our compulsion to know what others are thinking, and our craving for a bargain. Separately, each yearning is compelling. Combined, they're irresistible. The odds tell us what's in fashion, and what it costs. What else matters?

How we play the odds defines us. We are as we bet. Favorite players are cautious, front-runners, Republicans. Long-shot players are dreamers, skeptics, anarchists. Many inhabit both camps, often simultaneously. To bet a favorite is to feel reassured, but ordinary. To bet a long shot is to feel hopeless, but adventuresome. There's no escaping some residue of self-doubt, though. All in-between bets make you feel in-between.

Most bettors lengthen their odds as they grow older. They know favorites are overbet *because* they are favorites. One loses one's taste for beaten 4–5 shots after a while. You're a chump if your favorite loses. You're still a stiff if it wins. But you're a visionary no matter what your long shot does. Most bettors reach the point where they'd rather go for it, whatever *it* is.

Listen to this. Stop everything and pay attention. Don't watch the board! Stop looking for early action or late tickle. Stop believing in smart money. What is your money, stupid? It'll kill you. It'll make you crazy. You'll bet an underlay because it's the "hot horse." You'll bet an overlay because it seems to be on sale. You'll bet a horse at 20–1 you wouldn't spit at at 10–1. What is this, Crazy Eddie's? IT'S STILL THE SAME HORSE.

The horse is the thing. And the race. Not the numbers. Forget public opinion. Don't join it, or fight it, just ignore it. Don't lead a reactive life. Don't let them own your mind. It's philosophically unsound. It's for bozos. It portends ruin.

If you must watch the odds though (and of course you must), here's how to do it. Mix fundamental and technical analysis. Don't bet a good horse at a bad price, or a bad horse at a good price. Bet the best horse, but only at a reasonable price. Make your choice before you even see the odds. Set the minimum price you'll bet it at, and stick to it. You'll have to be patient; many of your choices will be bet down. But this is the way the great gamblers bet. It's the real angle.

It's also boring.

So here are two other angles:

Bet the longest shot with any chance at all. (Just imagining it winning is worth the two bucks.)

Or play all the 9–1 shots.

They're my lucky odds.

ODDS BOARD *Keeneland, 1985*

Classic

We seek perfection.

It could appear today, or tomorrow, or the next day. News of a fresh candidate floods the track. No one speaks of anything else; it consumes the place. An unraced two-year-old who could be "any kind." That's what we're looking for, "any kind."

Racetrackers bet against unbeaten horses reluctantly. Any one could be *the one*. It hasn't disproved itself, remains unblemished, potentially *it*. We stand in awe, await developments.

The classic horse won't be merely a great horse. It will be something else again, will possess a quality we'll only recognize when we experience it.

History abounds with the almost. We've had close calls. Though the greater hopes, as always, remain to be seen. Trainers always have a better one in the barn.

Great horses are intelligent and self-possessed. They don't get beaten. The classic horse will be this, and much more. It will have speed and stamina, an elegant head, a lithe body. It will do everything effortlessly, yet with passion. It will be above all enigmatic, beyond category.

Of course it's fictional, a notion better dreamed of than realized. If we saw it we probably wouldn't recognize it, or admit it. Anticipating the vision is what keeps us coming back.

Apprentice

THE KID.

Steve Cauthen at seventeen, deep in his apprentice season, the best any American jockey ever had.

Cauthen was probably born to it. His father was a blacksmith, his mother a trainer's daughter. He grew up on a farm in Walton, Kentucky; hardboot country.

He worked summers at River Downs, rubbing cripples, walking hots, watching, listening. At four every morning he would enter his father's barn, straddle a hay bale, practice his technique. After dinner he watched patrol films, searching for clues.

After high school, he went straight to New York, got an agent, got mounts, won with them, like in the movies.

He won six million dollars his first year, six races in one day three times. He took the Kentucky Derby at first asking, won the Triple Crown with Affirmed, made the cover of every magazine. He was what apprentices dream of being.

The racetrack apprentice system is remorselessly feudalistic. Kids quit McDonalds to take a stab at it. They're athletic and small, have ambitions and illusions. They spend two years mucking out stalls, polishing tack, breaking yearlings. They quit. They come back. They stay. They learn to ride, maybe.

When the stewards think they're ready, they get a mount. They also get a weight allowance, which is their edge. They get ten pounds through five winners, seven pounds through thirty-five, five pounds the rest of the year. It's a powerful incentive for trainers to use them. Trainers will kill to take weight off a horse.

Each apprentice has one year to prove himself. It's a pitiless contraction, a cruel parody of juvenescence. If he creates a stir, he has a shot. If not, he's shown the door. There's too much competition to coddle marginals. The day the apprentice loses his weight allowance is the day the trainers stop calling. He's just another journeyman. It's a harsh lesson in entrepreneurial Darwinism, and in the accelerated aging process of athletes.

Most apprentices fail quickly. Hundreds try for every one who sticks. The rest lack skill, or resolve, or contacts. Something. Everything. Though something is enough. It's a task you must be great at to be good at. Those who aren't are washed up at seventeen.

When an apprentice is as complete as Cauthen, though, he seems to be reinventing the very thing he is learning. He appropriates the track. All considerations get filtered through his presence; in tribute to his skill, but even more to his promise. Collective nostalgia grips the disenchanted—for their own youth, for youth in general. Apprentices look impossibly young, even younger than they are. They could be someone's child.

These pictures capture the perfection of Cauthen's emergence— of blue heaven with a twelve-month warranty. They also capture the contradictions of his character, all the paradoxes that allowed him to short-circuit his boyhood. Like all prodigies he looks both intimidating and vulnerable, a parody of self-possession, a boy dressed up in a man's character.

He is standing in the midst of everything, yet he couldn't be more alone. He has the face of a flawless waif, yet his expression betrays his knowingness. He seems flexible, yet steely; engaging, yet aloof. He could be a guileless farmboy, or a scheming Botticelli acolyte. He may be contemplating the mysterious power in his fingertips, or counting the days remaining to his year.

STEVE CAUTHEN ON THE BACKSTRETCH *Saratoga Race Course, 1977*

STEVE CAUTHEN IN THE PADDOCK *Saratoga Race Course, 1977*

Journeyman

THE TOP HAS ROOM for few riders; a dozen maybe, plus fifty more in the affluent second tier. Several hundred others make a decent living. The remainder keep their day jobs.

How a rider apprenticed, and where, seals his fate. It's not a forgiving profession.

If he made a splash in the big time, he may stay there. If not, he drops a notch, then another, until he finds his level, somewhere he can win. If he failed in the bushes, he's failed, period. He can't move lower—he's already there. Few apprentices ascend once they're journeymen. Fewer survive shaky beginnings. It's as good as it gets that first year.

Great riders levitate on technique, guts, charm. They have a sense of the horse, and of the problem. They are relentless in pursuit of what's necessary. And they have great hands. All agree it's in the hands.

Merely competent riders must cultivate a knack—for grass riding, for front-running, for something. How the rest survive is a mystery. Enigmas abound.

Some spectacular apprentices collapse as journeymen. Some mediocre beginners keep getting better. There are talented riders who can't buy a mount, and terrible boys everybody uses. Go figure.

Where they are says how they're doing. Great jockeys stay on one circuit, leave town only for big races. Middling riders shuttle regularly from track to track, following a trainer, or an agent. Bad jockeys move continuously, seeking a place where they haven't failed yet. Some second-raters prefer winning occasionally in the big time. Others like headlining in the sticks. The money's the same; only the rewards differ.

We follow them down, intrigued at their decline. It's like any bad life story, any imaginable fate. Where will it end? Will we eventually see them riding at the fairs?

Most jockeys collapse precipitously. They're as ephemeral as television weathermen. They just disappear, leave no forwarding addresses. Perhaps they resurface at lower levels, perhaps they don't. Scanning the *Racing Form* one morning we come across their names. We're shocked; we'd forgotten they even existed.

Surface appearances rarely suggest compelling reasons. They may be lazy, or crooked, or obnoxious. They could drink, or get homesick, or go crazy. They gain weight, or lose interest. Ambivalence, as it's wont to, intervenes. We'll never really know. It's privileged information, seldom shows.

Millions of small men dream of becoming jockeys. A few do. Here are portraits of some. All have survived their own apprenticeships, and the apprenticeships of hundreds of others. All have surfaced on the far side of the imponderables.

ANGEL CORDERO *Saratoga Race Course, 1978*

93

CASH ASMUSSEN *Saratoga Race Course, 1981*

PAT DAY *Keeneland, 1985*

JULIE KRONE *Monmouth Park, 1986*

JOSE SANTOS *Saratoga Race Course, 1994*

Equipment

THE HORSES WEAR THEIR SHOES, and nothing else. Although ingenue grooms sometimes lace their manes with flowers.

Little is added on race day. The bridle is placed over the head back at the barn. The bit goes between the teeth, like a retainer. The reins hang absently from the shoulders. In the paddock, the saddle is added. It's comically tiny, just a sliver really, bandaged to the back. Newcomers gasp at it. A numbered cloth is placed beneath it, for identification. This cloth has several pockets for holding weights. The stirrups are aluminum, never iron. That's it. Except for problem horses, which get blinkers if they're distractable, tongue ties if they're anxious, shadow rolls if they see things that aren't really there.

The jockey's equipment is equally sparse. The whip is just a slender reed, with a rattle at its tip. The horse hardly feels it. It's the sound that focuses its mind. Jockeys sometimes carry their whips in their teeth, to facilitate hand-switching, to make themselves look cool. The goggles are plastic, single lensed. For mud races, five or six pairs might be required. They're stacked over the eyes, in layers, then discarded as they're soiled. Extras are often given to children as souvenirs.

All else is uniform.

The helmet is fiberglass, covered by a cloth Eton cap. The post-position number is cardboard, affixed, garter-like, to the arm. The boots are leather, sleekly crafted, as dainty as any dolly's. The livery is the "silks," the trademark of the craft.

Individually colored silks were introduced in 1762, at the New-market course in England, "For the greater convenience of distinguishing the horses in running, and for the prevention of disputes arising from not knowing each rider." Nineteen different colors were chosen by nineteen different owners. Most were appropriately muted. The Duke of Ancaster settled on buff, the Duke of Bridgewater held out for "garter blue," and Mr. Jenison Shafto, to hardly anyone's surprise, picked pink. The "straw" motif, selected by the Duke of Devonshire, is still in his family, the oldest racing colors.

Every stable may design its own silks. It's a challenging task, but eagerly undertaken. Other than naming the horse, it's all most owners get to do. Variations in taste are afforded great latitude. Clashing colors are much in evidence, as are stripes, polka dots, flags, symbols, in-jokes, monograms. The line is drawn at indelicacy and advertising. Veteran racetrackers revere the classic motifs: the black shirt and cherry cap of Wheatley, the yellow field and grey braid of Rokeby, the devil red of Calumet. It's the descriptions, as much as the hues themselves, that captivate. It's hard to imagine "devil red" surrendering the lead.

Every track has a tailor who sews silks. Most will play couturier for a fee. Silks cost about $125 a set. Several sets of each owner's are kept in the jockeys' room. Valets fetch and return them between races. They're no longer cut from actual silk, of course. As befits the current drift, they're now nylon.

DRESSING FOR THE RACES *Northampton Fair, 1985*

Weight

HORSES MUST CARRY assigned weights during races. Jockeys who exceed such weights annoy trainers, and have their indiscretions announced to the crowd. Overweight is a handicapping factor.

Jockeys who want to earn a living must "make" 115 pounds, tops. For tiny riders it's no problem. For larger jockeys it's a nightmare.

Laffitt Pincay, Jr., has won more money than any other rider—more than $100,000,000. He was the leading money winner from 1970 to 1975. He's already in racing's Hall of Fame.

In the early 1970s, Pincay began taking one diet pill a day. They frayed his nerves and troubled his sleep, but they helped control his weight. A few months later he added a water pill. They gave him cramps and made him dizzy, but they forced the liquid from his system.

Soon neither pill was enough. He began spending an hour every day in the steam room. He bought a hot box for his home, would sit all morning in it, watching game shows. He had to lose five pounds every day to make 115. He became enraged when the sweat wouldn't come.

His diet grew increasingly ascetic: a glass of water for breakfast; a bowl of bran, one cracker, and tea with nothing for lunch; a bowl of soup and a baked vegetable for dinner.

In 1974 he collapsed in the Aqueduct jockeys' room. He had no water in his body, no salt, no potassium. The emergency-room doctor told him he'd die in a year, that his heart would explode.

But Pincay wanted another riding title. He couldn't stop. Soon he was dizzy all the time, had the shakes, hallucinations. Anemia thinned his blood. Parasites invaded his spleen. He woke every morning thinking, "Do I have to go through all this again?"

Then his best friend, Alvardo Pineda, died on the track. Everything stopped.

Pincay fired his agent. He cut down on his mounts. He devised a new diet, of nuts and seeds and bran. He began emphasizing the races he won, forgetting those he didn't. His weight stabilized at 117.

Soon he was no longer the top money-winning jockey, he was just *one* of the top money-winning jockeys. He was still punishing himself; he just wasn't killing himself anymore.

The rewards are always visible, the prices less apparent. Jockeys must fight everything: age, rootlessness, danger, each other. Weight is the final straw. They eat grudgingly, induce vomiting, gobble laxatives. It's a 365-day-a-year obsession. Fat never sleeps. Watch them when they mount the scales after a race. They eye the needle with an anorectic's occlusiveness. They could probably name the number to the ounce.

This is the steam room—before the races, after the races, between the races. It's where some riders live. The figure on the left is no rider. The riders are over the masseur's shoulder, losing the same pound they lost yesterday, and the day before that—spare curiosities struggling to accentuate their anomaly, tiny men trying to get even tinier.

STEAM ROOM *Fair Grounds, 1977*

Injury

Tim Haire started riding at seventeen. He won sixty races in three months, then broke his wrist in a fall. He was out for five months, but still won 200 races as an apprentice.

The next year he got flipped in the gate, fractured a neck vertebra, lost all sense of balance, was out for seven months.

When he returned, a horse shattered a leg and fell on him. The field trampled them both. Haire broke three more vertebrae, five ribs, suffered internal bleeding. The doctors said he'd never ride again. He was riding again in eleven months.

His fourth fall broke his back and pelvis, paralyzed him for ten days, disabled him for a year. He was beginning to get discouraged.

As soon as he returned, another horse threw him, fracturing yet one more vertebra, putting him back in traction.

"That's it," Haire said to no one in particular. "I'm retiring."

He got a job as an official at Waterford Park.

Naturally, he came back. His retirement lasted nineteen months. He couldn't bear not riding, not at twenty-nine.

Haire's case is hardly exceptional. Jockeys die on the track, during races, and during training. All get injured, all the time. They shatter limbs routinely, sacrifice spleens, discs, superfluous cartilage. Between traumas, they endure the indigenous wear and tear: bowed legs, curved spines, stretched tendons, calcium deposits. It's no normal position they've adopted. Even uneventful rides are grueling. Apprentice jockeys often can't walk after their first race.

Anyone who's sat on a horse can imagine. The ground looks so far away, and so hard. Horses are powerful and willful; when they move the perils multiply exponentially.

Anybody who's seen a thoroughbred can't imagine. Skittishness is their trademark. They could do anything, and often do. Add in the race's abrupt circumstances, and the odds become prohibitive: enormous animals with wired nerves and broomstick legs, running at breakneck speeds in tight packs for substantive purses. Their tiny jockeys often seem Scotch-taped to their backs, hanging on for life.

The dangers are even greater now. New painkillers keep crippled horses running, the jockeys never know which legs are real. At the cheaper tracks, the risks are *beyond* prohibitive. The horses are sorer, the turns tighter, the jockeys dumber, the stewards laxer.

An accident on the track looks like nothing else. The horses are cruising along, and then they aren't. One crashes over suddenly, its legs disintegrate. There's no warning. It's like film snapping in a projector, or a café bombing. Absolute order is absolutely obliterated. The jockey flips forward and disappears. Other horses fall over him, or just miss. Jockeys are taught to roll into a fetal position, not to move. Those who witness such mishaps can't imagine anyone surviving. An ambulance sits on every track, discreetly camouflaged.

Jockeys who return after a fall nurse fresh perspectives. Often they're thought to be unnerved. Sometimes they are. Some jockeys never recover from the shock, from having their mounts, and their worlds, explode beneath them.

Why do they risk it? The obvious reasons: glamour, excitement, competition, the risk itself. All the things that bring the rest of us to the track. They might even make a million, who knows? It's not as secure as most jobs—which is another plus. To ride thoroughbreds competitively is to be slightly more than alive.

This is the jockeys' room, between races. Stripped of its silks, the body at risk displays its tendencies: broad shoulders, distended biceps, a neat scar running half the length of the arm. One jockey plays cards to kill the time. Another naps in the background, eyes wide open. Mayhem looms around every turn for them. They do their best to deny it their undivided attention.

KILLING TIME *Great Barrington Fair, 1978*

Characters

WASN'T IT FREUD (or somebody like that) who observed (in that way he had) that neurosis is just another word for personality—that to be slightly irregular is to be more than slightly human?

The racetrack doesn't create eccentrics, it attracts them. But it does little to curb their quirks once they're there. It fosters idiosyncrasies, encourages traits we'd tend to temper elsewhere. People become cartoon versions of themselves at the track. It's a license to act inappropriately.

You get inured to most of the incongruities. Individual kinks assume normalcy *en masse*. Then one day it all screams out at you again, the sheer volume of it, its pervasiveness. You suspect your own peculiarities might have gained the upper hand, that you've stopped seeing the characters because you've become one of them.

So you look around again, and harder. The variety of the distortion amazes. The anatomies all look shockingly askew, the attitudes all appear willfully bent. But it's the clothes that really cry out, "Get the net."

No unfortunate fashion fad ever disappears from the track. It's like an open-air museum of wretched low couture. You see plaid bell-bottoms you thought went out with polio, capri pants functioning as God never intended them to, petroleum by-product ensembles ordered from braille Sunday supplements. Nothing fits. Nothing matches. None of the colors exist in nature. People wear outfits to the track they wouldn't wear to flee a fire.

Unanswerable questions occur reflexively. Do any of these people own mirrors? Did they rise this morning intent on self-ridicule? Do I look, in any way, like any of them?

Even the richies seem inapplicably garbed. New money dresses Vegas. Old money dresses old. Half the clubhouse ladies seem to be wearing the dress the Duchess of Windsor was buried in.

The duds are just an emblem, of course, though their symbolism is all too eloquent. It's a roguish pastime; one must play the part. Few get barred from the track for impropriety. It's one of the last places where you're free to *be* your character.

These men capture the self-referential aplomb of the dress-up game perfectly. If you saw them in the real world you'd say, "Those are guys you only see around the track." When you see them at the track however, you don't have to say anything at all.

TRAINER IN THE PADDOCK *Saratoga Race Course, 1985*

GROOM AND HORSE *Great Barrington Fair, 1978*

Post Parade

THE RACETRACK is adamantly ritualistic, as immutable as a Coptic communion rite. The horses enter the paddock on cue. The jockeys assume their sternest expressions. Losing bettors round up the usual excuses.

Each gesture is repeated sequentially, by rote, race after race, year after year, in Trollope novels, in Manet watercolors, in the fifth at Yakima Meadows. Only the horses' names ever seem to change.

Such formality transcends ordinary repetitiveness. It is form adhering lovingly to function, pleasing esthetes and pragmatists alike, providing an anchor of certainty in a sea of ominous happenstance.

The post parade is the foundation of these rituals. The jockeys are tossed up into their saddles, like animate beanbags. The horses make a slow turn of the paddock. They walk, single file, toward the track. Grooms lead some, ponies others. A few accompany themselves. They step, in order of post position, onto the track. The bugler plays the call. The procession winds past the grandstand, turns, and heads up the track. At the finish line, the parade disintegrates, like a chain of restive molecules. The horses break into their warm-ups. The entire process takes five minutes.

It's designed to facilitate inspection. Sweating horses are assumed to be nervous. Front-leg bandages indicate soreness. Fractiousness means something, although opinions differ as to what. Is your groom confident? Is your jockey signaling someone? Does your horse somehow *look* like a winner?

In fact, the post parade is mostly tire-kicking, rubber-necking, another thing to do. It lets us get up close, feign expertise, sell our brains on what our hearts have already bought for us. It lets us participate in the ceremony.

This picture captures the civilizing effect of the post parade perfectly. It freezes the action, much as the ritual regulates it. Two red-jacketed riders lead; eight racehorses follow. Seven outriders. Three grooms. Single rows of bettors communing at both rails—closet traditionalists, like all tough customers. It is a memorializing of lines, and of order. The lines of horses. The lines of onlookers. Palms, paths, chairs, fences, shadows, history.

Held to the eye, this photo draws us immediately into it, comes alive with the cryptic turmoil of orderly life, the conflicting factions, the looming dramas. It has the mannered tension only ritual brings forward, the subtle distinctions only formula can make plain.

Style

THE RACETRACK is style on the half shell, an extraneous metaphor meticulously executed. It welcomes high-livers, and low life, then blurs the distinctions, creates an alloy. It is top hats and parasols at Ascot, porkpies and beehives at Aqueduct.

A gentleman adopts a certain style at the track: dignity without hauteur, earthiness without vulgarity, drama without a script. He knows the racetrack treasures boldness, deplores the middle ground. He affects a certain flash to signal his agreement.

A gentleman likes the following things about the track: the way the riders whistle to their horses in the stretch, the way a great betting day grows in myth in your memory, the way losing bettors stay in action without incomes. A gentleman likes the constancy of the form, the variety of the results. He likes the self-containment, the fantasy, the raciness.

A gentleman treasures such things, accepts them, wouldn't change them, makes no judgments. He knows their presence conjures up that most elusive of characters, himself.

A gentleman behaves a certain way at the track, neither soliciting attention nor ducking it. He doesn't wear a tie—that would be pretentious. He doesn't wear a John Deere cap—that would be common. He bets every race, to be sporting, keeps his companions informed, though not pedantically. He cheers, eschewing gentility; speaks softly, shunning boisterousness. He feigns neither boredom nor absolute knowledge. He calls horses by name, never by number.

A gentleman claps for exceptional performances, and for all his own winners. He watches the races live, never on television. He reveals his losing bets as well as his winners. He never flashes a bankroll, underplays cash. He bets partly by head, partly by heart, always on the nose. A gentleman acts instinctively, makes grand gestures, never whines.

More than anything, though, the gentleman acts himself at the track, or that particular self the track activates in him. He doesn't imitate to belong, never condescends, wouldn't substitute stance for stylishness if he knew how to.

The gentlemen in this photograph have racetrack style down cold. To certain types, they may seem nondescript—to those who confuse glamor with style, who never quite get it. But observe their absorption, their casual elegance, their lack of self-regard. They're at Hialeah, peering down into the paddock, watching the horses. They compliment, yet stand apart from, their surroundings. They are rapt, yet self-contained; participating, yet remote. To those never truly at home in any one part of this world, or of themselves, they are a lesson. They've found their particular attitude, their own harmonious middle ground, racetrack style.

SURVEYING THE FIELD *Hialeah Park, 1977*

Owner

ANYBODY CAN BUY A RACEHORSE. So anybody does. Queen Elizabeth, the Culligan man. Nowhere is athletic egalitarianism so apparent as in the walking ring. Old money rubs elbows with new money, and short money, and funny money. It's like a split week in divorce court.

You can spend $10 million for a horse, or $500. You can throw in with nine of your cousins and take a gelding from a dispersal sale. It's the cheapest entrée into professional sports. And it's convivial. The basic requirement has always been soul—the imagination to dream of horses, the resiliency to recover on awakening.

Only a fool buys a racehorse to make money. You buy a racehorse with money you can lose. And you do it quickly, before you do something foolish with it. It costs about $20,000 a year to keep a horse in training. Only a fraction cover expenses.

Here's what you get for your checks.

You get to hang around the shedrow annoying your trainer. You get to stroll into the paddock and be eyed enviously by the railbirds. You get to tell friends; "We're considering a minor stake at Monmouth for him later this summer." You get to call a prominent jockey "my rider." You get to hope.

There are books that explain all the intricacies of racehorse ownership—depreciation, dosage, that sort of thing. They make owners feel more responsible about their recklessness. Forget them. Here's the scoop.

Pore over hundreds of auction catalogues. Buy a bargain yearling with undetected qualities, evocative bloodlines. Hire a young trainer who looks like Jimmy Stewart. Design classic silks in bold, primary colors.

Go slow with your horse. Don't run it until its bones have set. Win a maiden race in the provinces at first asking, then an allowance race, then a stakes at the same track. Sneak up on them.

Ship to New York. Win the Hopeful in an upset, then the Futurity, then the Champagne. Become the talk of the track.

Lay up over the winter. Be available to the press, but enigmatic. Win the Flamingo and the Wood. Resist pressures to switch to a more experienced jockey. Win the Kentucky Derby (as the favorite), the Preakness (on the front), the Belmont (going away). Take the Travers in August, then ship to Europe for the classics.

Win the Arc de Triomphe and the Irish St. Leger (they're run the same week, but something can be arranged). Become the toast of Europe, self-deprecating, yet self-contained. Turn down a $50 million syndication bid. What a sportsman!

Run your horse at four, to give something back to racing. Tour the country, to give the people a chance to see him. Run on the grass, in the mud—do it all. Finish with a come-from-behind victory in the Jockey Club Gold Cup. Steal away quietly, undefeated—the dream horse, and its dream owner.

The man in this picture is owner concentrate. His tie and cigar shriek déclassé. His suit and hat murmur cavalier gentility. His demeanor could mask any attitude. His trainer seems to be his groom. Nobody in his employ is making eye contact. It doesn't matter. He's beyond all approval. He's achieved the ultimate racetrack goal. He's standing in the paddock next to HIS horse.

SADDLING TREES *Saratoga Race Course, 1975*

Demographics

THREE BLACK GROOMS, watching a white crowd, watching a Puerto Rican jockey.

Many blacks work on the backstretch: elderly southern gents with courtly airs, quiet island men permanently dazed by displacement. They're cheap labor, and rarely transcend it.

Many women work on the backstretch, too. They've fallen for horses, in books, in boarding school, on farms. They've come to play out their unrequitedness. They're valued for their touch and their attentiveness, but rarely promoted.

All ages and regions colonize the shedrow. Drawls predominate, even among the northerners. Above all, it's a working-class environment. Even society trainers are careful to drop their *g*'s.

Horseracing is a surprisingly exclusive world, for all its surface egalitarianism. It's white, male, conservative; as formally organized and rigidly regulated as a Basque political sect. Alliances are pivotal, as are vendettas. Racetrackers are loners compelled into packs.

Women rarely become trainers. Blacks rarely become anything. The absence of black jockeys is *the* abiding mystery. There was an outbreak of female riders a few years ago, but it's since subsided. Latins are the ascendant minority. They're traditionally horsemen, native cabalists, have iron butts.

The gambling mix is equally diverse, though less conspicuous.

Most gamblers are older. They've got some money, and much time. They came up when it was more the thing to do. On weekdays, in the gray months, the grandstand becomes an oldies club, full of smoker's coughs and sensible shoes, of bifocals held three inches from the *Form*.

All races are represented, though some more liberally: Passionate risk-takers (Italians, Arabs). Meticulous risk-takers (Orientals, Anglos). Fatalistic risk-takers (Irish, Jews). Solitary Chinamen are the reigning cultural cliché. They inhabit countless corners, in their white Van Heusens and no-color suit coats.

The most notable lines are drawn around gender. Most gamblers are male; almost all plungers are. Women rarely go to the track alone. It's primarily a male escape, like power tools.

Caste isn't a factor. The rich just bet more, and stay nearer the clubhouse. Nobody goes to the track to get wealthy, just to be right.

One other sociological quirk leaps out at you—an inordinate number of the regulars seem defective. On the backstretch you see limps, hear stammers, shake withered hands. In the stands wheelchairs are common, and crutches, and false limbs. It's a safe harbor for all sorts of outcasts. And for dreamers. Because dreaming is the track's lone demographic constant. If this fault can be combined with *physical* deficiency, so much the better.

The horses don't mind.

WALKING RING *Saratoga Race Course, 1978*

Start

TWICE PAST THE GRANDSTAND, the post parade dissolves. The jockeys rise in their irons. The horses break into canters. All are free now to warm up individually.

Most of the limbering occurs on the backstretch, beyond our gaze. We monitor it through binoculars, noting the distinctions. Obstreperous horses worry us, as do stoics. The line between eagerness and hysteria grows finer. Equanimity is often read as indifference. Every tic takes on potential significance. We accumulate the evidence, make of it what we will.

Sometimes a horse bolts during the preliminaries, throwing its rider. Unexpectedly liberated, it makes like sixty up the backstretch, heading for its barn. Loose horses always point straight for home, as we'd like to. They rarely make it. Outriders position themselves preventively, make rodeo-style interceptions. The horse is led back toward the gate in disgrace. Its rider, equally mortified, regathers his dignity, and his courage, and remounts.

If the horse has overtaxed itself, it is scratched. Its backers get refunds. The odds rearrange themselves, always downward. If no harm seems done, the episode is dismissed—except by those who've bet the horse, who now consider themselves the deadest meat imaginable. There are surely cases of such horses winning, but who has seen one?

Two minutes before post time, the field reassembles. It moves slowly toward the gate, from the back, in stately procession. At major tracks, races go off promptly at post time. In the bushes, procrastination prevails. Somebody might have some money left to bet.

When the horses reach the post they just stand there, posing for immortality. It's one of the track's most arresting tableaux. Horses enter the gate in order of post position. Problem horses are often left to last. Some go in nice as pie. Others require coaxing, nudges with the whip, a locked-arm lift, a blindfold. The acquiescent just stand in the gate, waiting.

The loaders are beefy and phlegmatic, bouncer types. It's all they do. The starter oversees them, like a cowboy, or a grandpa. He stands on a platform just inside the rail, shouting instructions through a bullhorn. He has to get every horse in, settled, faced forward, ready to run. It's a demanding job. Few do it well consistently. Horses are often turned sideways when the doors spring, riders are left clamoring for assistance. I once saw a race start with three horses *behind* the gate. Starters who avoid such calamities can keep their jobs forever.

Once in the gate, the horses tense. The assistant starter holds his red flag aloft. The bell rings along the betting line, shutting the machines. The crowd grows quieter than it's ever been before. You'd think the pope just walked in. The jockeys sit chilly, squeezing the reins. This is the most dangerous time. Jockeys get killed now. Horses rear, crushing skulls against the grillwork; large fields bump boisterously as they're sprung; awkward horses have the ground give beneath them.

It's also a tactical time. Tenths of seconds lost here are never quite regained. One must be ready, to get the jump, to get position. When the starter presses his button, one must be off.

Nothing moves now—horses, riders, bettors. Time stands still, suspended in the gate. One second, two, three, four, five. Then, suddenly, they're . . .

Here, the last horse is being led into line. His seven opponents await him. The footprints document the task. The jockey adjusts his chin strap. Two loaders rush to calm an insurgent. An enigmatic figure, in raincoat and binoculars, observes impassively.

POST TIME *Saratoga Race Course, 1978*

Track

WE GO FOR YEARS, but never see it, never *really* see the track. We notice the buildings, the Fotomat facades, the last-ditch interiors. They vary. The tracks all seem the same. We take them for granted, like any road.

In fact, each course has its own endearing variables.

There are two surfaces: dirt and grass. Dirt predominates in this country. It's speedier, and cheaper. Many American tracks don't even have grass courses. Those that do tuck them inside their dirt strips, like afterthoughts. Most of the world runs on grass, considers dirt racing another American barbarism.

Tracks vary in configuration also. Cheap tracks are tiny, half-milers. Horses who run on them are always on some turn. Most tracks are an honest mile around, though Belmont is a mile and a half. The horses look like Raisinettes on its backside. European tracks aren't geometric—they wander all over the place, take various paths, disappear charmingly from scrutiny. The horses run clockwise on most of them. Their surfaces undulate; several furlongs often head straight uphill.

Textures deviate wildly.

Some dirt tracks are bouncy, some dead. Some grass courses give, others are unyielding. Dirt tracks have alternating layers: gravel, clay, sand, soil. They're stacked, torte-like, to facilitate drainage. The number of levels and their thickness dictate character. Western tracks are thin-skinned and sunbaked. They produce three-percent faster times than eastern tracks. Northern tracks are sandy, moisture absorbing. Loamy tracks are kindest to the legs.

All the bettors care about is the track's condition *today*. It's updated on the infield board all afternoon. A "fast" track is dry, a "good" track drying. "Sloppy" tracks are covered with water, "muddy" tracks have absorbed it. "Slow" tracks were drenched, "heavy" tracks were drenched and drenched again. Turf courses inspire similar labeling, but separate adjectives: "hard," "firm," "yielding," "soft."

Some horses prefer the mud. It's an angle even nonbettors know about. But all mud isn't necessarily equal. Sloppy tracks look most forbidding, but are fast underneath. Heavy tracks appear dry, but play like mucilage.

Even less attention is paid the mythic variables: topology, climate, ambiance. Certain horses prefer certain tracks. Nobody knows why.

When we get up close, we see some surprising things: how sensual it is—not flat, as viewed from postcard range; how vast its dimensions are, how wide, and how long; how much a world of its own it is; and how little of it comes into play. We notice the furrows left by the watering trucks, the stones turned up by the motorized rakes. We see horseshoe prints by the hundreds, air pockets by the thousands. We see how real it is, and how elusive that particular reality still makes it.

THEY'RE OFF *Suffolk Downs, 1986*

Race

MILLIONS OF THEM, at thousands of tracks, for hundreds of years, over and over, all alike, none the same—like sonnets, or seasons—the form immutable, the detail *sui generis*. The constancy charms us, the diversity intrigues. It's an irresistible composite, the invariable sheathing the arbitrary. It keeps us turning the page.

The horserace is a costume drama, a miracle play. Beginning. Middle. End. Consider the six-furlong sprint, the generic American contest. It has the unwavering conformation of the classic three-act tragedy.

Or farce.

The gate snaps open, raising the curtain. The horses spring to their task, set the scene. You'd expect them to begin uniformly, but they rarely do. The first jump brings critical distinctions. One always hits the ground running, as if notified beforehand. Others commence grudgingly, as if soft on the whole idea. The rest sort themselves out accordingly.

They reach full stride in seconds, for hundreds of yards just accelerate. Then the positioning begins. Front-runners hug the rail, hoarding ground. Contenders aim to stay within hailing distance. Latecomers try to stay out of trouble. Riders have to know their horse's style, and that of their opponents, and act accordingly.

By the half-mile pole the race has assumed its character. One horse seizes the lead, or several try to. They want to slow the pace, conserve their energy. Closers hope for a speed duel. Quick fractions might force the front-runners back to them.

At the turn the hardest decisions get made—to let it out, or save a little. The jockeys do a quick read of the situation, on the pace, on what's under them. Veteran bettors can name the winner here.

Then they're around the turn and into the stretch. Last act, flat out. Jockeys flash their whips, scream encouragement, withhold nothing—there's nothing to withhold anything for. The wire is in sight. It's now, or it's never.

The stretch run takes only moments, but presents endless possibilities. The leader may draw off. Two horses may run as one to the wire. A latecomer may circle the pack, coming from nowhere. Some horses will pull up on the lead, fearing solitude. Others won't pass to begin with. Many horses make a career out of finishing second. Great jockeys steal races in the last jumps, pumping rhythmically, dropping that nose *right on the wire*.

Route races are the same, only longer.

Here are four horses struggling to be first. We're at the top of the stretch, the place of asking. The horse on the right is leading, but not for long. His jockey is already pushing too hard, bent double. The horse outside him is about to intervene—he's eager, cheeky, envisions no obstacles. The horse on the left has both of them measured. He knows how fast he's going. It's faster than them. The gray horse is further back than he looks. But he's rolling. Certainty lines his eyes. His rider has spotted an opening on the fence. They're going for it.

TOP OF THE STRETCH *Suffolk Downs, 1986*

Rooting

We take all our selves to the track: our hopeful self, who likes to dream, our skeptical self, who doesn't, our philosophical self, who reconciles the two. During the race all these selves convene, plus some others. The race enthralls us, distracts us from our poses, allows us to be our *one* self momentarily.

Turn away from the horses then; face the stands. Watch the expressions, the emotions. You'll be alone in this; it's a private showing. Dead features become suddenly pre-orgasmic. Hope leaps from one face to the next. The race gets run in them. It's like watching a stranger's life pass before him.

Rooting styles betray us at the track. We become who we are when the world isn't watching.

Some jump up and down in place, unable to stifle long-deferred optimism. Others sway hypnotically, incapable of giving any hope a voice. A few wave their arms, pushing their horses, making the race (in their minds at least) participatory. Fingers are snapped. Feet are stamped. Programs are crushed into little cones of worry. It's all indelibly personal, parimutuel performance art.

Verbal styles are mated to the physical. Doubters assure themselves they're "looking good." Pedants instruct jockeys to "push that goddamn horse." Doomsayers criticize every move that's made. Nervous wrecks stare at the floor, but request updates. Latins shout. Wasps murmur. Women implore. Men insult. Chanters repeat one mantric phrase from flagfall to finish: "Come on seven. Come on seven. Come on seven. Come on seven. Come on seven. Come on seven. Come on seven. Come on seven . . ."

Deeper conclusions can't be drawn from rooting styles. Nor can you imagine what your own might be, unless you listen.

Here's mine:

Encouragement to the half-mile pole, exhortation to the stretch, recrimination to the wire. My favorite pronouncements are: "He shouldn't be *there*." "He hasn't asked him *yet*." And "Go to them with that horse, *Georgie boy*." I always scream at jockeys when I'm excited, usually by first name. Ardor breeds my familiarity at the track.

From this photograph, several conclusions may be drawn. The horses have just made the turn—each expression has achieved that level of intensity. Five men watch the race on television. Two observe in real life. A cowboy checks the placing board for numbers.

Each face reports a different race. The second guy from the right is gaining contention; he's getting revved. The man with the mustache is trailing; he's begun rooting against his discards. The fellow biting his nails is leading—that's how you feel on the lead, *any* lead. The guy with the binoculars is dropping back, his smile has turned decidedly upside down. The cigar smoker is still hoping, he still has a shot, just not much of one. The kids with the ties are laying third, anticipating a rally. Like most dignified participants in this exercise, they seem a little unfamiliar with the people they've become.

TURNING FOR HOME *Keeneland, 1985*

Edge

EVERYBODY KNOWS SOMEBODY who beats the races: a second cousin, a bowling partner. They're an irritating mythological constant, like the shoeshine boy who bought Xerox for a dollar.

Of course nobody *really* beats the races. Those who claim to only devalue the quest, make a mockery of every honest plunger's torment.

Details of their technique prove elusive. "I don't know how he does it, I've never been to the track myself. I think it has something to do with algebra."

Nor are obvious discrepancies ever subjected to scrutiny, such as: "If you've beaten the races, how come your Nova's still up on blocks?"

Those who tell, as usual, don't really know. Although to feign omniscience is forgivably human. Those who claim to have beaten the races have done so, in their way.

It probably was once possible to make a living at it, before usurious takeouts stacked the deck for good. Now the track skims seventeen percent from every bet. No gambler alive can beat a seventeen-percent edge.

Still, many live to try, like the "bridge jumpers" who bet five-figure sums on prohibitive favorites to show. Can such zealots really be called professionals though, just because they bet so heavily, and so often? Doesn't professionalism presume a certain profitability? Is living to bet the same as betting for a living?

All the professional gamblers I've known have had night jobs, or trust funds. None was named Johnny Dollar. Few owned a cummerbund. They were lonely, detached men who lived sad, claustrophobic lives. They had no social skills, and one obsession. Perhaps some did succeed. But I doubt it. I haven't.

Which of the gamblers in this picture is the serious one?

Not the guy with the Indiana Jones decoder ring. He conforms too dutifully to the type—too much chest hair, too many Macanudos. Devoted gamblers don't advertise their raffishness, or have enough leisure time to shop for virgin cashmere. This gent suggests a retired restaurant-supply salesman from King of Prussia, Pennsylvania, free finally to play his daydreams to the hilt.

It's not the wry preppie, either. Many penny-loafer types have sought sanctuary on the track—law-school refuseniks, career black sheep. This guy isn't one of them. He's not crazed enough. He's combed his hair this week. He's less enthralled with the track than permanently bemused by it.

It's certainly not the woman. Women have better things to do.

Nor is it the road-show hard guy, biting his Viceroy 100. Nobody in a "Magnum P.I." T-shirt has ever raised a stake.

None of the players in this picture is a professional, actually. But if one was, he'd resemble the guy with the glasses. This is what professional gamblers look like, I'm afraid. Like ex-violin-prodigies who live with their sisters; like lonely computer programmers who collect Peter Nero albums.

It's a disappointment to everyone, of course, most notably to the professionals themselves. But who else would pursue such a regimented dream life, a fantasy more constricting than any reality it might be compensating for?

STRETCH DRIVE *Santa Anita Park, 1986*

Steeplechase

STEEPLECHASING IS horseracing hyperbolized.

They jump barriers, over long distances. Aside from that, everything seems about the same. Little is. These distinctions make all the difference. They make it another sport.

A few jumpers also compete on the flat. Most are specialists. It's a singular talent. Horses who've botched everything else often master it. Jump trainers keep an eye out for prospects.

Some chase stables also work the main track. A few society owners keep token jumpers, feeling ancestrally obligated. Other outfits race only jumpers, horse-show types, Volvo station wagons, paisley bermudas.

Steeplechase riders only take the jumps. They're often tall, cello-bow thin, rarely "make" 135 lbs. Some are Irish exercise boys, others are hardboot farmers' sons. Most are daredevil rich kids, biplane aces. They're blond, with opaque skin and plumb posture. When they enter the paddock, it's like a fire drill at Choate.

Only three states still run jump races at major tracks—New York, New Jersey, and Delaware. One race a day, a few days a week, a few months a year. To survive, steeplechasing has formed its own circuit—small country courses all along the Eastern seaboard. Each hunt meet runs one weekend a year, April to November, with five to seven races daily. Purses are miniscule. Only two conduct betting. It's "good family fun," *trés gentil*.

In Europe there are tracks just for steeplechasing. It's a going concern. Real people work at it, and bet on it. In this country, it's regressed to hobby status, charmingly anachronistic, another vanished splendor. The common horseplayer won't bet on jump races. He thinks betting on anything that can fall is for suckers. Actually, steeplechases are the most formful of races. But you can't tell the common horseplayer that. You can't tell the common horseplayer anything.

The steeplechase world is the subculture's subculture, a sealed universe within a closed system, rarified almost to the point of self-parody. Those who run it are both endearing and infuriating, with their mixed-doubles manners and their numb-nuts noblesse oblige. You could kiss them for this wonderful thing they treasure, kill them for the airy way they treasure it.

The sport itself is beyond beautiful, and perilous in every aspect. Spills occur routinely, though more riders are hurt than horses. They go hurtling through the air and land on their cocoas. They lie motionless, awaiting the ambulance, like little gentlemen. They've always just broken something, or are about to. Fear doesn't seem to be an issue.

Stand in the old wooden boxes at Saratoga some perfect August afternoon. Watch the steeplechase field parade onto its course. When they hit the grass, they bound off through the infield trees. It's an almost imaginary moment. As is the instant when they burst from the tape, take the first jump collectively, flow as one down the backside, fly around the flags into the stretch. You can't capture it, can't explain it, can hardly stand it. It seems almost not to be happening. It's like the absolute idea, ideally realized. You want to freeze it in its sublimity, prevent it, in whatever way necessary, from disappearing.

LAST FENCE *Fair Hill, 1986*

Regions

THE WORLD IS DIVIDED into two precincts: countries that have racetracks, and countries that don't. Racetrackers visit the latter reluctantly—not because they don't have racetracks, but because they're the *kinds of places* that don't have racetracks.

By racetracks, of course, we mean thoroughbred tracks, not quarter-horse tracks, or harness tracks, or, well, dog tracks. Such places aren't really racetracks. We're not sure what they are.

Racetracks exist in countries you'd never dream possible. Only four really matter: the United States, England, Ireland, and France. Three others almost matter: Canada, Italy, and Germany. The rest make various efforts.

There seems to be no pattern to any of this. Except that tracks exist wherever Britain has ruled, but in no countries lacking a major sense of humor. There are no tracks, for example, in either Iran or Angola.

In the United States, racetracks are randomly dispersed, in exactly half the states. A roster only confuses.

Internationally, the competition is between the U.S. and Europe—for top horses, for bragging rights. Europe has the tradition. The U.S. has the money. The stylistic differences are conspicuous. Europeans run only on grass, over distances, clockwise. The jockeys ride high, seven races every afternoon. The horses move from track to track daily.

In the United States the tracks are dirt, the races short. Meetings last an infinity, or several months. The better stables follow a seasonal circuit—New Jersey to Florida, for example, or Maryland to Louisiana. The horses go where the action is; the horsemen accompany.

Even within a state, regional differences apply. The great tracks tend to be near large cities. Marginal areas can support only marginal racing.

Bettors are the same everywhere.

These are working class ethnics in the grandstand. The rich ethnics are in the clubhouse, wearing ties. It's the same in every country, every town. Exiles haunt the track—Tunisians at Chantilly, West Indians at Newmarket, Puerto Ricans at Aqueduct. They feel at home there, with their countrymen, with the horses. The surroundings may differ, but the racing itself remains basically the same, region to region.

WATCHING RACE ON MONITOR *Santa Anita Park, 1986*

Regulars

To PURITANS, gambling is *the* unpardonable sin. Their smiles freeze at its mention. Better to admit to child molestation. It's a secondary benefit of going to the track.

For such people, money is the nonpareil; it has icon status. It's to be earned, saved, invested. Certain amounts may be spent appropriately. None may be gambled.

Justifying this prudishness comes easily, usually in the form of cautionary tales: of uncles forced onto welfare by the track, of partners who tapped the till to play the ponies. They've seen the destruction gambling causes; they've seen the suffering.

Who hasn't? It doesn't hide. It flaunts its profligacy. Still, it has nothing to do with the track. Compulsive gamblers are compulsives before they're gamblers. The track's just where they hang their hats.

You see them everywhere—pacing the lawns, drinking alone in the Futurity Lounge. They're easy to spot; it's in their eyes. They stare, dart, stare again, slightly crazed, irrevocably committed. You could set fire to their pants, they wouldn't notice. They've burrowed into themselves, fled the graph.

Part of us despises their loss of control. Another part envies their escape from it. They've tied the can to conventional encumbrance.

The draws are obvious: it's a game, it seems beatable. It's liberating, yet formulaic. It doesn't keep shifting under your feet, like life. The risks are artificial, supplanting real risks. It's sexy, but demands no contact. Then there's the fresh air, the instant results, the outlaw ambiance. It doesn't even have to cost much—just whatever you have.

When compulsives lose (and they *all* do lose), why do they keep at it then? To punish themselves, as the conventional wisdom has it? Perhaps. But they also happen to like the place. And their luck could change at any moment. If they've gone to lose anything, it's themselves.

Here's my favorite degenerate-gambler story. It's also my favorite racetrack story, period. It sums it up, and has the added appeal of being true.

I was standing in line at a dreary New England venue one November afternoon, preparing to bet the last race of the day. An old man in a Salvation Army chesterfield approached me, clutching a single dollar.

Here is our conversation, recreated in its entirety:

"I'm down to my last buck, pal. Wanna split a bet with me?"

"On which horse?"

"I don't care."

LONGSHOT PLAYERS *Santa Anita Park, 1986*

Lingo

"BULL RINGS" are half-mile tracks. "Chalk players" are devotees of favorites. "Feathers" are carried by lightly weighted horses. Speedy horses display "early foot."

Gratuitous professions use jargon to justify themselves. The more extraneous the calling, the denser the idiom. The law has no peer at this. Legal verbiage translates freely into nothing.

Essential pursuits need no such smokescreens; they breed lingo.

Muddy tracks are "off." Sweating horses look "washy." Unruly horses seem "rank." Rural horsemen are "hardboots."

Many track terms have seeped into the parlance. Most are self-explanatory: "across the board," "also ran," "dark horse," "home stretch," "in the money," "on the nose." Others need interpretation. Jockey Edward "Snapper" Garrison invented the "garrison finish." "Morning lines" are the opening odds. "Walkovers" are uncontested races.

Racing vernacular is equine populism in tongues, vagrant street poetry as evocative as any quatrain. It draws on English saddle references, Western cowboy talk, and universal gangster argot. It states concisely what often seems beyond saying.

Suspended jockeys are "grounded." Former "maidens" have "graduated." Claimers are "platers" who run for "tags." Steeplechasers "jump up" over the "timber."

The shedrow is where horsey slang invents itself; it's rarely heard in the grandstand. Those who speak it there tend to sound a bit like tourists, like Sunday painters who smoke Gauloises and wear berets.

It's OK for anyone to talk it in private, though. And it's necessary to talk it to yourself.

The best track patois is both mysterious and revelatory.

Days with no racing are "dark days." Jockeys are given a "leg up" into the saddle. Tired horses "spit out the bit" because they're "short." Those who stay in the gate "refuse," or "dwell," or even "sulk." You slow a horse by "rating" it. You hurry a horse by "asking" it. Easy victors "win laughing" under a "hand ride." Slow runners "carry the target" and "never get a call." Willing horses are "generous." Calm horses are "kind." Consistent horses are "honest" and "hard knocking." Courageous horses have "bottom" and will "come again."

Some terms should never be used, but are. Certain bettors refer to horses by number, as in "the six horse." Others call inferior runners "pigs." Speaking like this makes milksops feel dangerous. Those who overhear them might actually believe they belong.

A few terms almost defy you to say them—words that fire the blood, make the pastime seem essential. A meeting's final races are run on "getaway day." Turf routes are contested at "grassy miles." An unbeaten horse might be "any kind;" wagers on it should be made at "any price." Triumphant beginners win "at first asking." "Getting" the distance is the ability to last it. "Win" means won, as in the past. The easiest of wins are won "as the rider pleased."

FINISH LINE *Oaklawn Park, 1981*

Finish

THEY LEAVE THE GATE with world-class intentions. Along the way something frequently gets lost: stamina, resolve, luck. By the sixteenth pole, inevitability has asserted itself. Some have stopped to walks, others are weaving in mid-pack. The wire can't come soon enough.

Jockeys develop a feel for the finish line. They don't need to see it, they know it's there. They time their rush to it, extracting the last gasp, sometimes more. When they hit the wire they relax their grip, rise reflexively, bend over their mounts, as though whispering in their ears.

The race is over, although the running continues. The horses bounce easily through the clubhouse turn, as in this picture, motoring down. Once again they're proceeding uncompetitively. A late-closer often takes the lead here. The occasional horse can't stop itself, it's too wired, and must be flagged by an outrider.

Once through the turn, most decelerate gradually. They feel the ground beneath them again, regain their standing. Now the race is *really* over. They take a few steps in that spirit, then pause, and turn gracefully. They begin loping back toward the grandstand, toward us, to unsaddle.

The jockeys' silks billow in the breeze then. The horses wheeze from exertion. They come rolling back in sweating twos and threes, tossing their necks, like a posse, or like chasers in an English hunting print. Once again you can't pick the winner—from its looks, or its position. It's all a blur now, it's just the field again.

This scene is rich with the poignancy of expiration. The race has just concluded, each horse has passed the line. The jockeys' backs are arched, the horses' strides are shortening. They're about to surrender to normalcy again, about to return to the ordinary world. But they're not ready just yet.

The track curves left, urging them on. Seductive detail emerges from the landscape: furlong poles, an undulating turf course, a meadow, trees. A farmhouse looms on a distant hill. One can imagine the horses heading for it, passing it, turning the race into a secession—gone for good.

Death

THEY DO IT BY injection—T-61, with a muscle relaxant. The brain dies in one minute. There is no pain.

It used to be done by pistol, a small-calibre bullet behind the ear. The report often startled the customers, and left gunpowder floating in the air.

A horse breaks a leg during a race—so conclusively that it falls, or subtly enough to leave it standing. The jockey jumps to the ground, tightens the reins, fights the panic. The crowd quiets. Grooms run on the track from every direction, tiny figures invading the fatal spot.

The veterinarian is summoned. If the injury isn't terminal, a brace is applied. The horse is carted back to the stable. Decisions are deferred. If the damage is irreparable, the injection is given. A screen is pulled around the horse, for propriety. Death occurs. The body is loaded into the horse ambulance, as in this picture.

Why?

Because thoroughbreds are bred for speed. Their legs are too thin to bear their weight. Two-year-olds are raced before their bones set. Dirt tracks are too hard. Sprint racing is too stressful. Speed, and greed.

Horses snap femurs on the lead, crashing to the ground as if poleaxed. They shatter ankles near the finish, and struggle to the wire on stored courage. Pasterns crack audibly in the stretch. Ruined legs dangle at crazy, tragic angles.

Not all horses die so violently. Old horses, unbreedable horses, difficult horses—all eventually face the needle by appointment. Some go to canning factories or tallow plants, as in the jokes.

Most are dispatched at the track, their corpses carted to municipal dumps for a fee. The process goes by various euphemisms: put to sleep, put down, destroyed. Racetrackers call it "going to the killers."

A horse wins some races when young, a few more in its prime. Nothing spectacular—just earning its keep. As the years pass, the infirmities multiply. Speed diminishes. The horse begins descending that ladder, changing hands, moving to cheaper tracks. The course is set, the days numbered. Eventually it can't beat anything. A decision must be made.

This is the code: don't let the horse suffer. Mostly it's observed. But much of the suffering is endemic. Thoroughbreds are victims of their usefulness, and their fragility. They are disposable. Many that once couldn't be saved after an injury now can be, but only if economics, or sentiment, dictates.

Various rationalizations cover our discomfort: thoroughbreds live to race, they live better on the track than most animals. It's all true, and beside the point. They do suffer. They do die. We turn our heads. We have to. We love the sport.

Gentlemen retreat to the men's room when a horse goes down—to avoid the ritual, to escape the crowd's dumb chatter. Doesn't everything deserve to die in private, and in silence? Gentlemen think so. Gentlemen think of quitting the sport at such times, but know they won't.

Nothing in this picture could be less appropriate. The plywood hearse. The burlap pillow. The frayed blanket. The chain. The fixed smile. The cold eye of death.

DEAD HORSE *Great Barrington Fair, 1978*

Inquiry

YOUR HORSE FINISHED FIRST. That doesn't mean you've won though. Not yet. Not here. They could still take it away from you, claiming foul.

It's always the least expected thing. You picked the best horse; it *must* have won fairly. You're busy congratulating yourself, reveling in your shrewdness. Then the announcement comes:

"Ladies and gentlemen, your attention please..."

Your heart freezes, crowd noises evaporate. The lights begin blinking on the infield board. You're in for a very punishing wait.

Inquiries are lodged by stewards, fouls are claimed by jockeys. Inquiries are usually serious, claims of foul can be. When both occur simultaneously, someone's screwed.

The patrol judges sit in little towers around the track, looking for trouble. When they find any they phone it in. Jockeys lodge complaints as they're weighing out. Patrol judges run no risk in tattling, it's their job. Jockeys think twice. There are fines for frivolous claims.

Before videotape, inquiries were confrontational, like parents' night at reform school. The accused trudged sheepishly to the stewards' stand; his accuser faced him indignantly, histrionically. The race was reviewed by anecdote. In close calls, elocution could prevail.

Now everybody just watches the replay, over and over, from every angle. Jockeys may excuse their actions, but can't deny them—it's all on tape.

Riders rarely foul flagrantly anymore. Most offenses are committed by the horses. They tire and bear out, they swerve leaving the gate, they revert to nature and do whatever the hell they want to. Riders try to stay within the law, working their intimidations through posturing and positioning.

The stewards' charge is clear: no horse may impede another's progress. Fouls must affect the outcome to be actionable.

No minutes drag more torturously than these. Few uncertainties evoke such wishful thinking: that they're less likely to disqualify a favorite, that the longer it takes the more likely the charge will stick, that certain claims spring from ongoing animosities.

The lights on the tote board keep blinking hypnotically, making handicapping the next race impossible. You try to, but you can't. Your mind is stuck. You're being punished for having a winner.

Then the roar comes. It startles you, though you've been awaiting it. The blinking stops. But what's your number? Where's your ticket? For a moment you can't remember anything. Then the announcer's voice unravels the confusion.

"Ladies and gentlemen, after reviewing..."

You're saved.

"Ladies and gentlemen, for interference..."

You're sunk.

You won, but you didn't. Or you didn't, but you did. It's worse than getting nosed, worse than finishing last. It's metaphysical limbo.

Punishment is swift. Your horse is disqualified, placed behind its victim, "taken down."

Disqualified riders wait several days for sentencing. Some will be suspended, usually for five days. It costs them. They can't compete while they're "set down." And their terms—called "days"— are printed in the *Racing Form*, like parole violators'.

These bettors are watching a disputed race being replayed. The screamers think the winner should have been disqualified. The quiet ones think so too, but don't really care. The smiling man wouldn't argue with any of them, and doesn't need to.

WATCHING THE REPLAY *Saratoga Race Course, 1985*

Aftermath

THE GROOMS LINE THE FENCE, waiting. The jockeys ask permission to dismount. They wave their whips perfunctorily at the steward's box. Consent is assumed. It's an old English custom, a formality.

It's over now, unsettles by its overness.

The jockeys toss their whips to their valets, hop off, reclaim their saddles. A scale stands beside each unsaddling area. All jockeys must tip it, holding their tack. If their weight isn't what it was, they're disqualified. This rarely happens now. But jockeys used to scuttle weight down the backside.

Here's where jockeys claim foul, or decide not to. Here, too, is where trainers ask their questions. It's postmortem time.

The winning jockey doesn't dismount immediately, but walks his horse into the winner's circle. Those awaiting him look like they just got the job. They're celebrating expansively, granting diffidence a holiday. They're the same cast from the paddock, plus the extras victory always flushes forward. They form a skittish semicircle around the horse, chortling, slapping backs, flashing win tickets. The groom holds the horse's head straight. The jockey assumes a Sears Santa smile. The local Am-Vet commandant hands the owner a trophy. The track photographer snaps the scene twice for posterity.

These are the photographs that line bars in marginal neighborhoods.

"Summer Bee. R. Milendez up. April 17, 1971. Tampa Downs. 5th race. 6 furlongs. 1:13.2."

The clothes worn in them seem never to have been fashionable. The haircuts are always slightly lopsided. They're like fading snapshots of somebody else's Thanksgiving. They're the real reason owners do it.

The winner is led off to the testing shed. His victims are already up the track. The horses for the next race pass them, completing the cycle. The official sign is posted. The payoffs hit the board. Winning bettors gasp in approval. Now it's history.

Only the grooms know how exhausted their horses are. They see the veins bulging, the heads dropping progressively lower. Horses know when they've been beaten. Many take it to heart. They return straight to their barns, are washed thoroughly, walked until they're cooled, then returned to their stalls. They'll be checked periodically, to see how they've "come out of it." Tomorrow they'll start pointing towards their next race.

This picture captures the full freneticism of the aftermath. It's like a market scene in a wall-length Tintoretto. Everybody is bustling, moving purposefully. Half the minds are already on the next race.

The victor, number five, is being ushered by his groom to have his picture taken. His trainer is looking at his legs. Number four has just been unsaddled. His jockey is telling his story. *His* trainer is looking at *his* legs. One horse is being unsaddled, another heads for home. The denouement is perfectly demonstrated here, in all its ritualistic stages. Even at the humblest tracks, the final letter is adhered to.

UNSADDLING *Northampton Fair, 1985*

Valet

OWNERS DON'T RETIRE, they have nothing to retire from. Trainers rarely retire, they keep it in their heads. But jockeys must give it up, usually sooner than they'd planned to.

Some jockeys ride into their sixties; a few keep winning past fifty. But after forty, their time is heavily mortgaged. Small injuries linger, weight clings. Their brains still grasp the transient openings, but their reflexes put the messages on hold.

This is the downside to athletic investiture. You get everything—you just have to have it home by midnight. No wonder jockeys hang on too long, staving off their premature deaths in miniature.

A jockey's afterlife options are inherently limited. Few are educated. All are small. They've spent their entire lives perfecting one narrow skill, mastering one environment. They know the score, though. They know the humiliations of growing old in a company town, of being superfluous where you once were essential. But where else can they go? Where else would they want to go?

The racetrack offers few electives. Top jockeys become stewards or assistant trainers. Average jockeys become valets.

Valets are the jockey's gentleman's gentleman. They lay out fresh silks, mend tack, wash goggles. They check weights, polish boots, brew Sanka. They're paid a fee per race, get small bonuses for wins. At the better tracks, they wear a kind of uniform—little officer's caps and matching tunics. They're servants, really. It's a sinecure.

There's something touching about all intramural solicitude, but there's something chilling about this particular form of it. It brings former heroes back to earth too violently, parades fallen idols before us as servile mendicants.

To see great riders sliding toward oblivion is not a pleasant sight. They turn up without warning in the provinces, riding long shots, and not successfully. All wear the fixed expression of the still-active has-been—quiet pride mixed with melancholy sheepishness. "Get lost" seems kind advice on such occasions.

Even after they retire they haunt the track. You see them under the grandstand, looking lost, acting tentative, pining. They've added a paunch, a few wrinkles, decked themselves out in Sergio Valente Boy's Boutique. They seem suddenly inappropriate to almost everything, like aging midgets, like Ginger Rogers. At first you're glad to see them. Then you're not. You start averting your eyes. You want to shout at them, drive them from the track with little sticks. Where's your dignity, you want to ask them. Don't you know you shouldn't be *hanging around*?

VALET, JOCKEYS, TRAINERS *Keeneland, 1985*

Excuse

HORSES DON'T TALK, and they're notoriously poor listeners. So losing jockeys must make their excuses for them, and take their heat.

The moment the beaten jockey crosses the finish line, his brain begins assembling defenses. Hecklers are gathering around the unsaddling area. Disappointed trainers are streaming from their boxes.

In most cases, blame is easily dodged. Each race can have only one winner; most losers were expected to lose. Only when a big favorite dixies, or a jockey errs egregiously, does the grumbling threaten to escalate into hysterics.

Rush to the rail on such occasions. The floor show is well worth the trot—especially at eastern tracks, where jockey-bashing has become a minor folk art. It's like open-mike night for amateur character assassins.

Most of the glibbest knockers are regulars, guys who like to yell where yelling doesn't cost you. The one-timers are characterized by their lunacy—that sputtering rage that says: "I just blew the rent money."

The jockeys just take it, pretending not to hear. It goes with the territory. Though I once saw a thin-skinned journeyman vault a fence to coldcock a tormentor. My first reaction was one of primal incredulity, at seeing a tiny man dispose of a larger man so effortlessly. It jangled my already disheveled sense of the apropos. My second reaction was bitter disappointment, at having missed the crack that could elicit such an outburst. All misanthropes long to make such jibes their own.

Here's the best railbird brickbat of my experience, occasioned by the deep-sixing of a 3-5 shot by Angel Cordero:

"Hey Cordero, get cancer."

It's concise. It's vivid. It's specific. The imagery is unclouded by repression. It's poetry, really.

I was tempted to ask its author to elaborate, but I didn't want to intrude on his moment. And he didn't seem the text-embellishing type. Besides, I think I can fill in the blanks myself:

1) Inoperable testicular sarcoma.

2) Painful, lingering death.

3) An unmarked grave.

I've tapped out on a few 3-5 shots myself.

The abuse jockeys get from disgruntled employers is less visceral, but more substantive. Jockeys can be fired. Horses can't.

The jockey in this picture is twice threatened. By fan abuse (off camera, to his rear), and by a looming postmortem with his irate connections. The elaborateness of his shrug suggests more culpability than he's going to be able to defend.

The trainer, knuckles to brow, wants to kill himself. The owner, scowling, wants to kill the jockey. The son-in-law, bearded, is reserving judgment; but not really. Both daughters are sympathetic, but fear gunplay.

It's a riveting little drama, no less powerful for its pervasiveness. At the racetrack, most judgments made are faulty; as many as possible must be laid off on surrogates.

JOCKEY'S EXCUSE *Keeneland, 1985*

Maxims

"YOU CAN BEAT A RACE, but you can't beat the races."

Betting aphorisms are racetrack truth encapsulated. Who cares if they're clichés? Clichés are true. Only our familiarity with them breeds our contempt.

Yes, you can beat a race. No, you can't beat the races. But this adage says much more than that. It counsels moderation, the picking of spots. For addicts, it's invaluable advice. For dabblers, it's unnecessary. Part-timers aren't out to beat the races. "If they can run it, I can bet it" is their motto.

The accuracy of racetrack saws should reform us, but never does. Knowing and doing rarely run as an entry.

"They all get beat if you run them often enough."

"Weight will stop a train."

"Horses for courses."

"Money makes the mare go."

"It's not a beauty contest."

"Jockeys don't win races, they lose races."

All summarize a world view in one stroke. My two favorites are the two I've known the longest:

"First horse to the paddock, first across the line."

This is an old Irish epigraph—which means it's not really prophetic in the sense that it's actually going to happen. Still, it happens often enough to make it seem it happens more.

"Gray horses for gray days."

This literally means that gray horses, like that pictured here, run better in the mud, like that pictured here. It's sort of true, if you get my drift. Figuratively, it means just about anything you want it to, which is its real charm. It's also a lovely phrase to have tripping over your tongue at any moment, and the perfect truth to tell the perfect girl the first time you take her to the track.

Fixing

IT'S EVERY NEWCOMER'S FIRST QUESTION:

"Are they fixed?"

They've always assumed they were—heard it from uncles, read it in the *Enquirer*. It's a universally shared scrap of conventional wisdom. Frogs give you warts. Nuns are lesbians. Horseraces are fixed.

Consider the evidence: the cheap suits, the brassy attitudes, the sense of too much money chasing too little virtue. Consider the testimony: of gamblers rationalizing losses, of outsiders feigning insides, of Allen Jenkins' dialogue in Mickey Rooney movies. Presumptions of fix have something for everyone.

A subtle erotic burr colors the question—the lilt Evelyn Waugh called "the bat squeak of sexuality." If the races aren't fixed, they're going to be interesting. If they are fixed, they're going to be *dangerous*.

"Of course they're fixed," you tell them. "Isn't everything?" Such evasions satisfy no one. You fall back on the truth. Some are. And some aren't.

Mostly, it's a matter of money. At the big tracks everybody's making lots; they won't risk it all to cop a little more. At the small tracks, even the successes are failures; $1,500 purses make fixing almost mandatory. At the medium-sized tracks, fixing is a sometime thing. Here the traditional variants hold sway: character, greed, who's watching.

There are two ways to fix a race: buy the jockey, or hit the horse. You buy the jockey with blandishments, money being the blandishment of choice. You hit the horse through its bloodstream, orally or hypodermically. You can buy one jockey or hit one horse per race, usually the favorite. Or you can go for volume. By doubling up, you multiply both chances—of cashing your bet, and of getting caught.

Here are the most common types of fix:

A groom jabs a favorite an hour before post time. His confederate bets hundreds of exacta combinations, excluding the hit horse, which checks in a groggy sixth. This is called "stopping" a horse.

A guy in a green silk shirt pays the jockeys of three favorites $2,500 apiece not to "persevere" (as it's called around the steward's stand). He bets the other horses. This is called a "boat race."

In the most common type of fix (a type so common it's a handicapping angle at the dingier venues) a trainer instructs his rider not to persevere in a $10,000 race. His horse runs last, looking terrible, even lame. A week later the trainer drops the horse into a $7,000 race and lets it run; it trounces its inferior opposition, at a big price. This is called "pulling" a horse.

The stewards are supposed to keep an eye on the jockeys. The chemists actually *do* keep an eye on the horses.

After every race, the winning horse and one or two others (a beaten favorite, a washed-out also-ran) are taken to the testing barn to give specimens. It is this man's job to catch their urine. His method is simplicity itself. He places his mitre box in the appropriate location. He whistles. (It seems to speed the process.) He waits. He whistles some more. He waits some more. Most horses require only minutes; strong-bladdered horses can take hours. Obstinate horses sometimes last overnight. This man must stay at his post.

The results go to the laboratory, where they're examined for depressants, or stimulants, or prohibited painkillers. When any are found, purses are redistributed, trainers suspended. The parimutuel results stand, of course. The bettor, as usual, is out of luck.

URINE COLLECTOR *Fair Grounds, 1977*

Win/Lose

THERE'S ONLY ONE WAY to win at the track.

The number of losing methods seems infinite.

You can get nipped at the wire, or left at the post, or trapped behind horses. Your jockey can break a stirrup. His mount can break a leg. You can be eight lengths up and see your money jump the inside rail.

On May 26, 1966, I bet a horse named Taunton in the May-flower Stakes at Suffolk Downs. Taunton was leading by open daylight, in mid-stretch, when a recently discharged mental patient ran onto the track. Taunton swerved to avoid him, broke stride, and finished second.

I hadn't figured on Thorazine levels as a trip factor.

Reactions to race results are equally eclectic. Doping out a long shot is the best. Having a favorite disqualified is the worst. Getting nosed makes you feel almost smart, but victimized. Bailing out is like saving yourself from drowning. It's nice to share a winner with a friend. It's better to lose a little than a lot.

Stripped of detail, winning resembles life; losing, its opposite. Not that you can always tell the viable from the terminal. Many bettors mask their emotions, even from themselves. Some winners feel like losers, and vice versa. They don't let little things like the evidence affect their attitudes. I'm a pessimist myself. Yet I always expect to win. I can lose fifty in a row and feel sure I have the next one.

Losing at the track evokes grief in all its stages: denial, anger, sadness, resignation, acceptance. Winning works the same, only inside out. It's an exorcism ritual, an acting out of gain and loss in effigy. Triumph may be celebrated, loss dismissed as symbolic—unless you want to take your setbacks literally. The track honors all such requests.

These guys look like everybody on the subway leaving the track. Their jauntiness has been bludgeoned into submissiveness. They're out, but not down.

Still, there's one winner here. One of six, the usual ratio. It's not the guy on the left. He's too grudgingly detached. He has the expression of someone who could spray a 7-Eleven with machine-gun fire, then get himself a manicure. This is someone who's just taken a very hard loss. He either got off a long shot he loved, or dropped a bundle on a tip from his brother-in-law. He's tapped out, less than zero.

The man next to him is an aggressive loser—crisp, rational, self-contained. He's the only one here who got dressed with the lights on this morning. He's lost seven in a row, but he's got a hot horse in the eighth. He's going to end it all right there.

The gent on the right is nursing a long losing streak. He hasn't picked a winner since Roosevelt's second term. Losing streaks make you look like this, even make you feel like this, like you've forgotten where you live. They put you in a different category entirely. Everything you do feels wrong before you do it. It's like swimming in circles in the dark.

The man next to him is a disbelieving loser. He keeps checking his *Form* to see how this could have happened to him. When he finds a reason, any reason, he'll be able to go on. He'll be reassured.

The guy with the crutches is a generic loser. He expects it, doesn't take it personally.

The lone winner is the man with the cane. He's the only one talking. Repeated losses produce silence in the victim, remove the starch, like a series of sharp punches to the nose. Winners, on the other hand, love to talk, seem to need to, to share their ascendency, to explain their acumen. They have to be discreet about it, though. Ostentatious winners make losers want to kill them. Solitary winners seek out strangers to engage. Telling someone makes it feel a little realer, keeps the adrenaline pumping in tandem with the tongue. What good is winning, after all, if you have no one to bore to tears about it?

BETTORS RESTING *Keeneland, 1985*

Stooper

WHEN YOU BET on a horse you get a ticket as your receipt. If you win, you cash it. If you lose, you toss it away. By the last race, losing tickets blanket the landscape.

Pari-mutuel tickets used to be visually engaging, pasteboard rectangles, two inches by three, color coded by denomination, and intention. Two-dollar win tickets were a sybaritic yellow, ten-dollar combinations a golf-sweater blue. Fifty-dollar show tickets had the half-hearted chartreuse tint of store-brand pistachio ice cream. Calligraphic symbols covered them, to discourage counterfeiters. They looked like shoe receipts from an art-deco cobbler.

Now they're just computer printouts, on nondescript paper, resolutely mundane—like Teletron tickets to an Andy Williams concert. You don't get separate stubs for separate bets anymore, either—they squeeze them all on one, like at Safeway.

Even so, they're still *our* tickets, tangible evidence of our momentary venturousness. We treat them accordingly. Some clutch them throughout the race, for luck. Others ask companions to hold them, for luck. Two on a ticket negotiate joint custody giddily, or diplomatically. The cautious stick them in billfolds, the distracted in pockets. That's my tactic. But which pocket? Pockets seem to multiply at the track. Having a winner sends me rummaging through hundreds of them, convinced my luck has slipped again through some loophole.

It keeps the uncertainty perking long after the race, as it's intended to.

Every year, thousands of winning tickets go uncashed at American racetracks, millions of dollar's worth. It's a once-a-year sidebar in every big-city tabloid. Most are simply lost, or discarded in error. A few are kept as souvenirs. The rest go to nowheresville, with the number-two pencils and the unrequited argyles.

This man is a stooper. He's turning over discarded tickets, hoping to find a live one. He may, though I know no one who ever has. Most stoopers are children, interested more in volume than in quality. Adult stoopers tend to be less focused, and less hopeful. Few actually *stoop*. They turn single tickets over with idle toes, in the spirit of having nothing much better to do.

Serious stooping is a loser's game, played by the ragtag. They operate principally after the crowd has left—there's more room then, and fewer prying eyes. It's the racetrack equivalent of scavenging for beer bottles, or combing deserted beaches with rented metal detectors.

The floor in this picture was once spotless. It will soon be again. Air blowers will propel the trash into jumbo plastic bags: programs, racing papers, beer cups, pizza plates, thousands of tickets nobody wanted, a handful nobody was apparently meant to have.

UNCASHED TICKETS *Santa Anita Park, 1986*

Getaway Days

MY PARENTS MET AT THE RACETRACK.

This is a key element in their story, in our family mythology, a central metaphor. It has never been explained in detail, of course, has always remained benignly emblematic, a mere starting point.

I'd often wondered about this—wondered if my parents' meeting was just a simple story, like any couple's meeting; a story which I, in my writerly way, had embellished into a metaphor, a romantic first line for any writer's biography:

"His parents met at the racetrack."

Or was there actually more to it? Was the way I'd come to think of it, undetailed, totemic, an intuition of some deeper significance, a beginning of an explanation?

I decided to ask my parents.

And they told me.

When my father graduated from high school, in 1935, he got a job at Suffolk Downs, at the hot-dog stand. He was there the day they opened. They were still painting the fences.

My mother often visited the track with her family.

Neither remembers the exact moment of their meeting, the incident. The floor behind the concession stand was recessed. My mother recalls the first time she saw the "hot-dog boy" standing on level ground. His height amazed her.

On their first date they went to see *Gunga Din*. After that it was mostly the track. They'd met there, it was already their story.

Hearing this now, I can almost see them there again, as I'd always imagined them: the pre-war girl in her gigantic picture hat, the depression boy in his baggy gabardine pants. They are whiling away the long, innocent afternoons at the track, the racing days.

The war ended it. My father was drafted. In 1944 they married. The next year I was born. For seven years they didn't go to the track, they couldn't afford to. When they started going again, very occasionally, it was the fifties. They were older, had begun living different lives, the lives I think of them living.

Buried in this story is the significance I'd always intuited. I would not exist if there was no such place as the racetrack. And my birth stopped my parents from going.

My first trip to the track was in the mid-fifties. I was nine, or perhaps ten. It was the Weymouth Fair, the bottom rung. We'd undertaken a family outing, much anticipated, fiercely organized. There would be rides, outlaw cuisine, a full day of undiluted dissolution. If horse racing was mentioned, I took no note of it.

Yet there we were, at twelve sharp, on the finish line, following a full morning of Tilt-a-Whirl and geek gawking, of sheep-shearing demonstrations and mustard-pickle panorama—the perfunctory 4-H rationales.

The racetrack was at the east end of the grounds, a half-mile oval with a sad little grandstand. From the paddock you could see the entire midway: double-decker Ferris wheels with pastel neon tubing, distracted carnies flirting with giggling farm girls, giant taffy-pullers twisting in endless suggestive loops; white-trash heaven.

I was given two dollars to lease my acquiescence. It wasn't necessary. I already knew I loved the place, the vast expanse of the track, the conspiratorial buzz in the grandstand. The fair was exciting. The track was thrilling. I took the deuce.

The idea was that I could bet with it, on any horse, keep my winnings, not complain if I lost. I loved the notion, though I knew nothing of gambling, how to do it, or why. I knew only that it involved this place, and these horses. It was what adults did when they acted like children.

Just as the first way you tell a joke is the right way, the first bet you make is made your way. It's how you're *meant* to bet, before you learn how you're *supposed* to bet. You spend the rest of your life trying to recapture it. Or shake it.

I didn't bet on the first race of course, little adult that I was. Nor did I hazard the second, or the third. What was I waiting for? Parental suggestion? Divine revelation? More likely I was waiting not to lose. I watched the grooms bring their horses to the paddock, watched the plungers line up at the fifty-dollar window, watched, waited.

In the sixth race I knew it was time. The horse was April Fool, the favorite. Did I know this? Or only sense it? I couldn't read the *Racing Form*, couldn't even decipher the odds. What made this horse *the* horse? Not his looks certainly, or his name. Perhaps I'd heard him being tipped in the walking ring, misread some handicapper's certainty as real certainty, as beginners will. I didn't hesitate. I bet two dollars on April Fool to show. Actually I didn't make the bet myself, being too short. My father made it for me. But he gave me the ticket to hold. Someone hoisted me dizzyingly aloft to watch the race.

April Fool won easily, leading every step. I never took my eyes from him, heard no other horse's name. He paid $2.60 to show. I put the two dollars in one pocket, the sixty cents in another. I left both sums where they were. I didn't want to bet again. I felt I'd discovered some pivotal secret, the clarity of which I might blur by pushing my luck. I spent the rest of the afternoon stooping for tickets, like a nine-year-old.

If I'd quit then I'd still be ahead. But I didn't. I couldn't. Who could? I'd won the first time. That's powerful medicine. Not that I thought it would always be like that. I just thought it always *could* be.

I remember few other details of the afternoon; just the thrilling vastness of the track, the coziness of the grandstand, the fervor of the crowd, and dreaming of it all for months and months afterward. It was like everyday life lived at fever pitch.

What I recall more vividly are its abstract attractions: the festive air of spectacle, the physical sense of contest, the challenge of beating a system, of pursuing communally that noblest of ideals: something for nothing. Plus the pervasive erotic element—the unknown, the tension, the danger. The idea that my family did this made any story possible.

When I recall this incident to my father he denies ever attending the Weymouth Fair. He's been to the Marshfield Fair, and the Brockton Fair, but never the Weymouth Fair. My father is not wrong about such things. For a moment I feel the metaphor physically threatened, done in by the banalities of misremembered detail. I must either shift the memory to the Marshfield Fair, or excise my father from it.

I decide to do neither.

Shortly after my first bet (in my memory at least), my Great Aunt Kate, my father's aunt, gave me a certain book, a discard from the library of the Saltonstalls, for whom my Great Aunt Kate worked as a seamstress.

This book was *The Godolphin Arabian* by Marguerite Henry, a fictionalized biography. In it the Godolphin, one of the foundation sires of the British turf, is rescued from death by a young Arab stableboy. They rise to prominence together, with ultimately dolorous consequences. On its final page, a page I always dreaded reaching, began steeling myself against in the very first chapter, yet also anticipated with voluptuously melancholy relish, there was an uncaptioned portrait of the two standing together, staring into the setting desert sun, as they had earlier in the story, before reality intervened. This picture always conjured up feelings of family attachment in me, feelings of affinity, and

its costs. It seemed like an allusion to a story yet unknown, a story of adherence.

I read the book a hundred times. It became *the* book for me. Slowly, inexorably, its qualities combined—the solitary boy, the perfect horse, my Great Aunt Kate, the Saltonstalls—all blended smoothly into the racetrack story, before I knew there was a racetrack story to blend into.

I didn't go to a *real* track until I was fifteen. In those days minors weren't allowed. Then one day, freed unexpectedly from classes (a power failure? a principal's death?) I learned that Suffolk Downs was holding "fan appreciation day." I quickly talked my mother into going, into sneaking me in as though I'd reached majority.

I disguised myself as my father, thinking his trench coat and soft hat made me look thirty, when in fact, they made me look twelve. We approached the grandstand gate with inappropriate confidence. The ticket taker wasn't fooled for an instant.

"Lady," he screamed, "this kid is about *fourteen* years old."

My mother was speechless. I was immobilized. I thought we might be arrested. But then the racetrack spirit, as it will, prevailed. The man behind me, buoyed by the antic richness of the scene, its screwy piquancy, said, "Aw, let the kid in."

Instantly those behind him took up the chant.

"Let the kid in. Let the kid in. Let the kid in."

The gatekeeper was adamant. He was *doing his job*. It wasn't right. I'd tried to fool him. On the other hand, my mother seemed like a nice enough lady. And nobody important was watching. He released me.

"OK kid. Go ahead in. *This time*."

The crowd cheered.

I was in.

I remember nothing else of that day, not a race, not a bet. The big thing was that I'd gotten in, gotten into the track. It was an adult thing to do, and also childish, and there you have it. Later the entire incident became part of the family mythology: "The day Brendan got dressed up in Dad's clothes and snuck into the track." It was my first entry into the story. I instantly sensed its appeal, and its power; its distortions, and its accuracy.

As soon as I looked like I *could* be twenty-one, I started going by myself. Right off I went in a big way—sixty-six consecutive days, still my record.

I slipped easily into the numbing routines of mechanical attentiveness, rising in the late morning, walking to buy the *Racing Form*, taking the early afternoon subway to the track. I had a night job.

I slipped just as easily into the alluring obsessiveness of the gambling, began noticing the covert characteristics it brought out in me: how I bet, how I won, how I lost. Overall I did lose, though not much. It didn't matter.

I also appropriated a horse.

I was standing in line to cash one sunny October afternoon, sharing the smug camaraderie of the win window, when I heard the man behind me stage-whisper to his companion.

"He looked like the old Business Deal out there today, didn't he?"

The "old Business Deal." It was all I needed to hear. Here was a story appropriate to my fantasies: of former eminence in tragic decline, of heroic struggle against incalculable odds. I'd clearly bought my way into this story with my bet on Business Deal. I was hooked.

I never looked up Business Deal's actual history. I just kept imagining it. It seemed better that way. He became my horse.

I bet him every time he ran, and usually won. Then I began noticing his patterns, and always won. I had him timed. People noticed. They'd tell me, "Hey, Business Deal is running again

tomorrow," or ask, "How's that horse you always bet doing these days?"

Then he disappeared.

At first I thought he was just laying up for a while. I was tempted to ask his trainer, or somebody else, anybody. But the longer I didn't, the more afraid I got to. I just put it off, and put it off, as I'd always put off the last page of my book. The truth is, I didn't want to know, because, of course, I already did.

When that meeting finally ended, numb, yet still wired, in desperate need of perspective, I gave myself a horseplayer's holiday. I began working on a system.

For weeks I collected countless charts, extrapolated endless statistics, worked every day on it. I was looking for "the way." I made many discoveries, uncovered many patterns. But none of them led anywhere. There was no "way." There were only ways. The story remained elusive, beyond control. The elusiveness of the story *was* the story.

My sole concrete memory of that period is of sitting at a folding card table, scribbling away at my calculations, looking up occasionally to see ghostly astronautical figures floating across the television screen. Men were landing for the first time on the moon.

Then I met a girl. We didn't meet at the track, though we might as well have. We went constantly. The track was the part of my story I featured to her. It seemed to fit.

She loved it, the track, the story. I loved taking her. It was like showing her where my mind and heart met.

I won all year, couldn't lose, had the best year ever, as seemed fitting.

We decided to go to work on the track, like in the movies, or in a children's book. We wrote a letter, outlining our ambitions, a coy beginner's letter, appealing to the beginner in all who read it. We sent copies to selected trainers. One answered, sympathetically, though not encouragingly.

So we took our case to the track, walked the backstretch, quickly hired on to a cost-conscious trainer, Al Culp, from Elgin, Texas.

Our job was to walk the horses, clean the stalls, pick the feet. We were apprentice grooms, $2.50 an hour, thrilled at the thought. We came over at dawn on the subway, worked until ten, ate in the track kitchen, took a horse to the races occasionally, went to the races even when we didn't.

I liked the idea. But the reality very quickly lost its charm. The insularity of the backstretch felt oppressive. Turning a fantasy into a chore felt cannibalistic. It seemed like something that would make a wonderful story some day, but wasn't one now.

We kept at it though, knowing each day might be the last. Finally, after two months, one day *was* the last. We quit. Part of the story had finally been refuted, had bumped up against its boundaries.

To make up for this, we went straight to Saratoga, stayed the whole month, played at being mythic sportsmen instead of anonymous drudges. We stayed in a small room in a big house on George Street, went to the track every day, bet every race, had an ideal four weeks. It was a perfect story, yet something about it had gone strange. Working at the track had depleted the story for me, had forced too much significance on it. Immersion in the betting life wasn't reversing this process, it was deepening it. It was just too much.

When I left Saratoga I knew it was time to go on to something else, to leave the story alone, to stop enlarging on it. I knew that if I didn't, I risked losing it entirely, draining it of its true meaning, plundering the allegory.

I wasn't meant to be at the track all the time, I now realized. I was meant to think of myself as someone who could be.

There have been many stories added since, of course, adjustments to the mythology, but just adjustments.

For that is the real story of the racetrack for me—that it cannot be, and should not be, entirely real. It has always been as much a story as a place for me, a collection of stories actually—of Arab stableboys and successful first bets, of sneaking in and getting hooked, of indomitable claimers and surefire systems, of how I once worked at the track, and of how my parents met there.

When you tell a story too often it loses its spontaneity, achieves polish, becomes, not a feeling, but a performance. When you live a story you bring the outside world into it, forfeit its legendariness, cut off your escape route. This particular story, true as it was, couldn't stand the rigors of repetition, or of excess tangibility. It would cease to exist for me then, in the way that mattered most, in story form.

POST-RACE INTERVIEW *Laurel Race Course, 1985*

Photographer's Notes

I STARTED GOING to the racetrack in 1973. Mostly I went to the local track, Suffolk Downs, home of hard-nosed horse players and low-priced claimers; but occasionally I ventured as far as Rockingham Park in Salem, New Hampshire or Narragansett Park in Pawtucket, Rhode Island, which has since closed. The next year I made it to Saratoga, a world apart with its strawberries-and-cream breakfasts and million-dollar thoroughbreds. I've gone back there every year since.

From my very first trip to the track, I knew I wanted to photograph there, but it wasn't until my second Saratoga trip that I began to do so. At first, it was just casual shooting between races. Soon photographing replaced horseplaying as my primary activity. I shot for magazines, for newspapers, and, mostly, for myself—and I began to dream of doing this book.

Whenever I could find the time, I traveled to different racetracks. Over the next several years, I visited about a dozen tracks across the United States. The trips varied from three days to two weeks, but my routine was always the same. Each morning I would get up early to photograph the workouts and the backstretch activity, and each afternoon I would shoot the action at the track. Only occasionally would I take the afternoon off and work on the *Racing Form* instead.

I pursued this book for several years, then shelved the project. I was busy with other books and teaching and hadn't yet found a publisher. While I continued to go to the track, I went strictly for pleasure.

In 1985, with Brendan Boyd's help, I decided to revive the racetrack project. The idea of doing a truly collaborative book appealed to me, particularly since Brendan took me to the track for the first time (although for reasons unclear to me, he denies this). Anyway, we have been going to the track together for many years now and share both an interest in, and a common perspective on, racing.

The book was published by Viking Penguin in 1987. It was well received, but it soon went out of print. Brendan moved to Santa Fe, Montreal, and eventually Paris. His home tracks are now Longchamps, Saint-Cloud, and Deauville. I stayed in Boston, making do with simulcasting at Suffolk Downs until the Saratoga meeting begins.

Last year, Greg Hamlin at Henry Holt agreed to publish this paperback edition. We decided to keep the book pretty much intact, but I couldn't resist the opportunity to change a few of the photographs. Some of the additions are recent shots, but most are older ones that have improved (in my mind) with the passing of time.

For those who care about technical matters, the early photographs were taken with Leica rangefinder cameras and Nikon SLRs. Now I use Canon EOS autofocus cameras and various point-and-shoot models. Films vary from Kodak Tri-X and T-Max (400 and 3200) to Ilford XP-1 and XP-2. I took all the photographs here in available light — mostly hand holding the camera, but sometimes using a tripod. Porter Gillespie and Andrea Raynor made the prints, using fiber paper (Ilford Multigrade or Kodak Polyfiber), under my supervision. We slightly cropped about half of the photographs.

Almost ten years ago, some friends and I purchased a New York-bred colt named Omar Khayyam for the paltry sum of $5,000. The trainer said that this was his "Belmont horse." We thought he was nuts. Omar never ran in the Belmont, but to everyone's amazement he competed in stakes company. He was voted New York-bred Sprinter of the Year in 1987, and chalked up earnings of over $300,000 before a foot injury forced his retirement. We promptly invested the profits in three more horses and they all lost money. I should say, they lost all *our* money. With that experience, I retired from horse ownership for a while. But last year a friend convinced me to buy a small share in a two-year-old filly named Our Gallavanting. She isn't much of a runner, but we have high hopes for our new two-year-old colt — Rolling a Seven. He may be our Derby horse.

Acknowledgments

THE AUTHORS thank the following for helping us with this book: Leslie Arnold, Michael Blowen, Lindley Boegehold, Andy Carpenter, Jean Caslin, Melissa Cohen, Lisa DeFrancis, Megan Doyle, Dan Farley, Robert Fierro, Amanda Freymann, Greg Galvan, Robert Garrett, Porter Gillespie, Greg Hamlin, Eileen Hepp, Jennifer Hill, Elise Katz, Jonathan Landreth, Lauren Lantos, Ruth Liebmann, Ann Meador, Richard McDonough, Mike McGovern, Lorie Novak, Elaine O'Neil, Kim Pease, Ridge Qua, Mary Reilly, Mark Starr, Diane Taraskiewicz, Madeline Tillotson, and Amanda Vaill.

Special thanks to Andrea Raynor for her tireless and invaluable help in preparing this paperback edition.

Portions of *Racing Days* appeared previously in *American Photographer, The Boston Globe Magazine, Boston Review,* and *Town and Country.*

Photographs from Racing Days have been exhibited at the Kentucky Derby Museum (Louisville, KY), the International Center of Photography (New York City), and Sperry's (Saratoga Springs, NY).

Support for the photographs came in part from a Project Completion Grant from the Artists' Foundation of Boston.

Thanks also to the management of these tracks, which granted access for the photography:

Fair Grounds, New Orleans, Louisiana
Fair Hill, Fair Hill, Maryland
Great Barrington Fair, Great Barrington, Massachusetts
Hialeah Park, Hialeah, Florida
Hippodrome Saint-Cloud, Saint-Cloud, France
Keeneland, Lexington, Kentucky
Laurel Race Course, Laurel, Maryland
Linzay Downs, Eunice, Louisiana
Marshfield Fair, Marshfield, Massachusetts
Monmouth Park, Oceanport, New Jersey
Northampton Fair, Northampton, Massachusetts
Oaklawn Park, Hot Springs, Arkansas
Santa Anita Park, Arcadia, California
Saratoga Race Course, Saratoga Springs, New York
Suffolk Downs, East Boston, Massachusetts

WINNER'S CIRCLE
Laurel Race Course, 1985

RESTING BETWEEN RACES *Northampton Fair, 1985*